YOU
NEGOTIATE
LIKE A **GIRL**

YOU
NEGOTIATE
LIKE A GIRL

Reflections on a Career in the

National Football League

Amy Trask
with Mike Freeman

TRIUMPH
BOOKS

This book is available in quantity at special discounts for your group or organization. For further information, contact:

Triumph Books LLC
814 North Franklin Street
Chicago, Illinois 60610
(312) 337-0747
www.triumphbooks.com

Printed in U.S.A.
ISBN: 978-1-62937-187-0
Design by Patricia Frey
Title page photo courtesy of CBS

"She's not a girl, she's a Raider."
—Gene Upshaw

CONTENTS

AUTHOR'S NOTE

There are rough words in this book. I did not use such language gratuitously or to be provocative. I used it in some instances because I believe it necessary to adequately recount a memory or share an anecdote from my years in the league. In other instances I used it to convey a sense of the environment in which I loved to work. If this language offends you or stops you from sharing this book with a young person you don't believe should read such language, I am sorry. I will note, however, that if you or such young person wish to have a career in football, such language is not aberrant, it is the norm.

YOU
NEGOTIATE
LIKE A **GIRL**

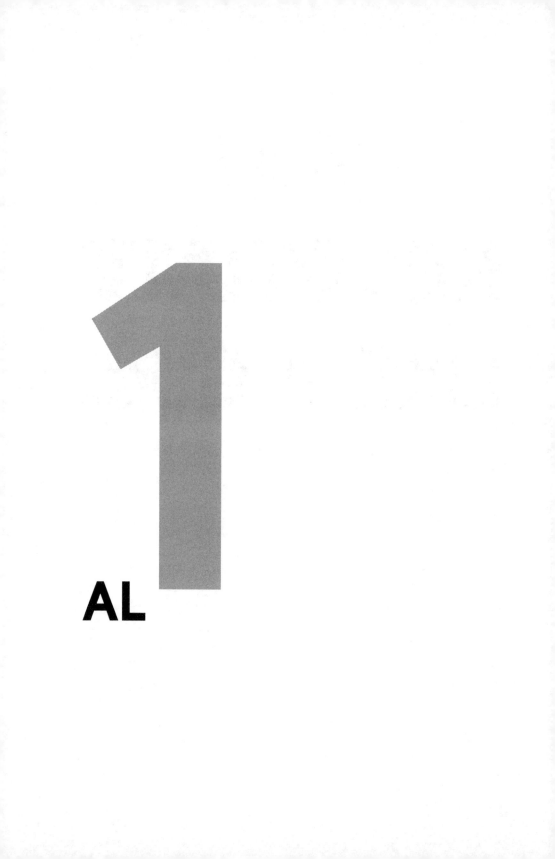

NEGOTIATING FOR AL DAVIS WAS A CHALLENGE. HE INSTRUCTED, he directed, he managed, he micromanaged, he bellowed, he denounced, he demanded, and he denigrated. On occasion, he offered praise and expressed sincere appreciation. Because those moments were far less frequent than the excoriating moments, they were meaningful and precious. I knew that when Al offered praise or expressed appreciation, he meant it.

One particularly crucial and complicated transaction that consumed us for a considerable period of time offers a good example of what it was like to negotiate for him. It was the most difficult transaction with which I'd ever been involved, by a large margin. (It may surprise some, but this transaction was not in any way related to franchise relocation.)

Al didn't like how or the pace at which negotiations were proceeding, and on one of the many occasions on which he shared his displeasure he declared: "You negotiate like a girl."

Al was tense and angry and irascible throughout this process and he made many other interesting remarks. At one point during a very heated argument, he said to me in a harsh, derisive tone, "You're like that emperor of Japan."

Now *that* pissed me off. That was substantive. I knew exactly what he meant. His insinuation of "unconditional surrender" was absolutely clear. I went to my office and made a big sign, which I taped to the door: EMPEROR HIROHITO'S OFFICE. I left it there for a month or so.

People were quizzical; a few asked me what that meant, and I told them to Google it. Ultimately, I took it down.

And the "you negotiate like a girl" remark? It didn't bother me.

People I respect have told me that I should have been offended by that remark and that I should have stated my objection to it.

I wasn't offended and I didn't state an objection. I knew that Al didn't care that I was a girl and I thought it a better use of my time and energy to negotiate and structure the most impressive deal possible.

So I rolled my eyes, laughed at him, and told him that he could handle the negotiation himself. Al responded as he almost always did: "Aw fuck." He didn't want to handle the negotiation; he wanted the girl to handle the negotiation.

I WAS HONORED THAT FOR much of the three decades that I worked for Al, one of the most enigmatic and extraordinary men in sports history, I was motherfucked every bit as often and every bit as forcefully as any defensive coordinator who worked for him. Certainly, those who knew Al knew that he motherfucked his defensive coordinators a lot. I was motherfucked every bit as much.

Swearing doesn't bother me – it never has. I swear a lot. Many have likened my choice of language to that of a truck driver or sailor, while others have noted that such comparisons are insulting to truck drivers and sailors. Perhaps I shouldn't swear as much as I do. A great Raiders tackle, Lincoln Kennedy, thought as much. Hearing me speak, he'd shake his head and laugh. He once told my mother and father after a game that he would like to work with them in an effort to clean up my language. They laughed and my father told him that they'd given up long ago.

There was one occasion when Al discussed swearing in front of a woman – or at one – that is particularly special to me.

We were hosting a meeting at our offices. Shortly after our guests arrived, and as a few of us were conversing with them, Al joined us. When he noticed that one of the visitors was a woman, he explained to her – and to the entire group, as all of the guests were listening to him – that he tried very hard not to swear in front of women. He apologized in advance if that were to happen.

Well, I began making overly dramatic, incredulous faces and looked from one coworker to another. They smiled back knowingly. Al then proceeded to explain to our female guest and her colleagues that while he might sometimes slip and swear in *front of* a woman, he would never – and did never – swear *at* a woman.

At that point I stopped dramatizing my incredulity; my escalating facial expressions and body language were organic. I gestured with my hands and the pen I was holding flew out of my grip and landed on the conference table with a thud. Everyone in the room turned to look at me, including Al.

"Well, Amy – I swear at Amy," Al said, "but I don't consider her a woman." *I don't consider her a woman.* Think about that. He didn't consider me a woman. Isn't that the goal? Isn't that the hope? To be treated without regard to gender? The moment was even more special than it would otherwise have been because in vintage Al form, he conveyed one of the most spectacular thoughts he could have ever conveyed, in a manner only he could: *Oh Amy – I swear at Amy – but I don't consider her a woman.*

I ACCEPTED MY FULL-TIME JOB with the Raiders in 1987 without knowing what I'd be paid. I was offered a job – I didn't ask about salary or benefits or anything – I just said yes. I walked down the hallway to the office of the managing partner at the law firm at which I was working and I gave notice.

I understand that not everyone has the luxury of accepting a job without taking into account financial considerations and that I thus did something that not everyone is able to do. I am not unaware of or insensitive to that reality. I was newly married and my husband and I were living in a roughly 400-square-foot apartment. Although we had financial constraints and obligations, I didn't think about them. I didn't care what I would earn and, as it turned out, I took a very significant pay cut to join the organization.

Some might say that what I did was foolhardy. I don't think it was. I wanted to pursue a dream and it never occurred to me not to accept the job.

Over the course of my career, Al periodically stated that not only should employees – including me – work for free, but that we should pay the organization for the privilege of so doing. It was my distinct impression that he wasn't teasing. No matter whether he was teasing or not, he believed it was a privilege to work for the Raiders, and so did I.

Just as I didn't ask about compensation or benefits before accepting my job, I didn't ask about career path, opportunities for advancement, employee reviews, or anything else that I was asked hundreds of times by individuals I interviewed later in my career.

I was offered the opportunity of a lifetime and I said yes.

At no time from the moment I accepted my job until the day I resigned decades later did I think about about my status or advancing within the organization. I didn't strategize, plan, or worry about my trajectory or next steps. I did my job. I did advance, but I never spent a moment contemplating, considering, or planning how to do so or whether I would.

It bothers me when people take a position already looking to advance. It struck me many times throughout my career that applicants and new employees were focused on advancement from even before they located the restrooms. Rather than focus on advancement, one should focus on doing the best job possible, on working as hard as possible, on working harder than anyone else, and on working harder than one ever thought one could. I was told many times over the course of my career that it was a failing of mine not to strategize for my advancement. I disagree.

Hard work matters. There is something to be said for being the first in and the last out. There is something to be said for doing anything and everything asked and for anticipating and doing anything and everything one can think of, whether asked or not.

On innumerable occasions, employees asked me how they could ultimately attain a position like mine, whether with the Raiders or another organization. I would often respond by asking, "Do you notice that when you get here in the morning, my car is already here? Do you notice that when you leave at night, my car is still here?" Most often that response was met with a blank stare. My words didn't resonate.

Do your job. Work hard. Work harder than you ever thought possible. Then work harder.

MANY PEOPLE KNOW ABOUT AL'S history, but not everyone does. Taking into account both his on- and off-field contributions, there may not have been a greater pioneer in the history of the National Football League. On the field, Al helped revolutionize the passing game, and he remains the only person to be an assistant coach, head coach, general manager, commissioner, and owner in the league. Off the field, Al also did revolutionary things. He refused to allow his teams to play in segregated cities, and he was inclusive in all regards, providing opportunities for many who had not previously been afforded such opportunities. Al hired, advanced, fired, and swore at people for decades without regard to race, religion, ethnicity, or gender. I am a beneficiary of Al's vision and openness.

There have been and still are many harsh criticisms of Al, some of which are quite fair, but even his most ardent detractors cannot, with a shred of intellectual honesty, question his record with respect to diversity and inclusiveness.

He was brilliant and tenacious, and we'd argue constantly. He was creative and combative, and we'd argue constantly. He was caring and infuriating, and we'd argue constantly. He was also funny.

At times his humor was dry and caustic and at times it was relaxed and silly, but it was always appropriate and well timed. There was one joke Al loved to tell and those who knew him knew it well: the Yum Yum Dog Food joke. Although I heard it countless times over many decades, sometimes in private settings and sometimes when he shared it publicly, I laughed each time, not so much at the joke, but at how much he enjoyed telling it.

A large number of sales representatives of a dog food company were gathered at an annual company meeting at which the president of the company was speaking. As he concluded his remarks, he built to a crescendo:

"Ain't we got the best damn dog food?" he asked the assembled employees.

"Yes," they cheered.

"Ain't we got the best damned sales representatives?" he next asked.

"Yes," they cheered.

"Ain't we got the best damned company?" he then asked.

"Yes," they cheered, now standing.

"Then why ain't we selling any dog food?" he asked.

"It's the dogs," one employee said. "They don't like it."

Al loved that joke.

"AW FUCK" WAS AL'S MOST frequent response to anything and to everything. He used this expression to convey anger, disgust, frustration, exasperation, compassion, affection, disinterest, and many other sentiments.

On one particular occasion, Al was sharing with a few of us his views as to what we should state publicly about a particular issue. I thought that he was utterly wrong, so I said, in a friendly yet sarcastic tone, "We'll get you your own Twitter account – you can tweet that yourself."

A moment later, a message appeared on my phone – one of my coworkers who was also in the meeting sent me an email that he would immediately register @awfuck for Al's official Twitter account. If anyone should have owned that account, it should have been Al. Then, he could "twit," which is how he referred to tweets when we spoke of them.

AL HAD A NUMBER OF other standard phrases:

"You don't know what the fuck you're talking about." If I had the proverbial dollar for every time Al told me that, I would be able to buy a team, or build a stadium, or both. This was Al's very clear, very straightforward manner of telling me I was wrong, which he did a lot.

"You miss the point." This was another phrase Al used to tell me that I was wrong. For decades I told people that were ever I to write a book, I would title it *You Miss the Point*, since he said that to me so often.

"Oh fuck him." This was Al's standard response when I shared with him that someone didn't agree with a position we had taken, that someone in the league office had communicated that we could not do something he wished, that someone was critical of the organization, or that someone had written or otherwise reported something unfavorable about the organization. Often, "Oh fuck him" was followed by some sort of additional insight, directive, or sarcastic observation or comment.

"You see it that way; I don't see it that way." I heard that a lot because we didn't see a number of things the same way.

"What I'm *tryin'* to find out." That was Al's not-so-subtle way of telling me that he wasn't interested in what I was saying, that he didn't like what I was saying, that he didn't want me to waste any more of his time, or all of those things.

"You're so negative." I heard this any time I pointed out flaws in a position he wished us to advance, offered reasons a plan might fail, or disagreed with his logic or reasoning.

"It's part of life; it's what you're dealing with." Part was pronounced "paht," of was pronounced "a," and life was pronounced "lahf." It's paht a lahf. That was Al's way of telling me that I had to accept something, whether I wished to or not. Al and I periodically debated whether we must accept something or not.

"You know how you are with words." I once asked him if that was his commentary on the precise manner in which I speak – he said *fuck* a few times, and then said, "Obviously."

"You're screw loose." That is how Al told me that he thought that something I said – or that I – was nuts.

Al had interesting ways of offering encouragement. "Hey, I didn't ask you to try, I told you to get it done." He said that to me the very first time he asked me to complete an assignment. One day during my first month or so with the organization, Al called me into his office and asked me to do something. When we finished our conversation, I said to him that I would try my best and as I stood up to leave, Al responded: "I didn't ask you to try, I told you to get it done." He was neither impressed by nor interested in my commitment to try; he wanted it done. Message received.

Also by way of encouragement, Al regularly offered what I referred to as his covered wagon story. "When those covered wagons got to the Rockies, Trask," he said, "most stopped, but some of those people were tough and made it through to the other side." He didn't want me to try; he wanted me to get my covered wagon through the Rockies.

"And try not to fuck it up." Al periodically offered that sage advice when he asked me to undertake a project. I believe that I started this tradition as it was I who first said to him, "I'll try not to fuck it up" after he asked me to do something.

Another favorite of his: "You must be slow, mentally." Only "mentally" was pronounced "ment'ly" – two syllables, not three. "You must be slow, ment'ly." Or, when he was speaking of someone else: "He must be slow, ment'ly."

"That guy, huh." When Al referenced, or when we spoke of, someone he did not respect or did not like, his common refrain was, "That guy, huh." He said it in a tone dripping with derisiveness.

"Fuckin' coaches" was another expression Al used quite often. Al and I began our first conversation the day after each game with a discussion of it. Whether we won or lost, Al always had some choice words for our coaches. There were more such words when we lost, of course. As we spoke of play calls, coaching decisions, player performance, in-game situations, and clock management, Al would routinely mutter, "Fuckin' coaches."

One time, when speaking with Al the morning after we lost a game, I commented on our special teams play and asked him if he agreed with my assessment that this was the primary reason we lost. He did agree and muttered "fuckin' coaches" a few times, referring to the special teams coordinator and the assistant special teams coach. I went on to ask him why we had chosen to block (or, really, *not block*) in a certain manner on our field-goal and extra-point attempts, since several of them were blocked. Al noted that he too wondered that (he didn't say it that politely, though) and that he had asked the special teams coordinator that very question. He then explained that the special teams coordinator told him why he thought our blocking scheme – in which we left one player on the opposing team unblocked and unaccounted for – would work. Al sort of shouted and sort of wailed, "Who asked him to think?"

Fuckin' coaches, who asked them to think.

Early in my career, many stadiums didn't have suites for the visiting owner. In those instances, Al watched from the visiting team section of the press box and I watched the game near him. (I didn't watch home games or road games in which there was a private area for him, with him. Well, not the entirety of those games; in those instances, I saw him prior to kickoff, during the game if I needed something from him or he needed something from me, and after the game.)

So in the instances in which he had no private area from which to watch, there we were, right smack in the middle of the media covering the game. One might think that because he was seated amidst the media, Al would have moderated his commentary on the game or at least the volume at which he offered such commentary. Nope. Al was undeterred by the presence of the media and he engaged in profanity-laced tirades when he didn't like something he saw on the field, often loudly slamming his hand on the desk when he did. I'd periodically whisper to him that his comments and actions were audible and visible and that he might want to moderate his comments or at least lower his voice so that they were not reported, and that, if he did not, he should not be surprised if his comments and actions were included in reports of the game. At times, I'd point out that it was apparent that the media were making note of his comments and actions. His response: "Aw fuck, I don't care about that." Then, the next morning, when we spoke, he'd express surprise and irritation that his comments and actions were reported.

Al was tremendously knowledgeable about world history and current events. He frequently crafted derisive nicknames for league officials, members of the media, and others and when he did so, he used his knowledge of history to manufacture some great ones.

After I shared with him the substance of some ongoing, difficult discussions with the then-CFO of the NFL, Al began referring to him as the gendarme. Although the term *gendarme* has a number of connotations, I knew from prior conversations with Al that he used that term in a disapproving sense, as a disdainful reference to French soldiers who served as an armed police force. For the rest of that official's time with the league, Al never referred to him by name, only as the gendarme. "What did the gendarme have to say?" he would ask me after I concluded a call with this executive. While other club executives criticized and complained about this gentleman, I appreciated his direct, forthright approach and that I always knew where he stood on matters; I never had to guess. Now that I think about it, those criticisms and complaints about him were akin to criticisms and complaints about me. I loved that Al bestowed upon him the name *gendarme* and I smiled every time he used it.

One of my coworkers bestowed upon one of the longest-tenured league officials the moniker Minister of Disinformation. Al smiled when he heard that one. Gendarme was my favorite.

Another name Al bestowed upon someone – and it amused him, a lot – was Dumbo. It was a name he gave a Bay Area columnist. Periodically, Al would ask me "what did Dumbo have to say about" something or other. I giggled each time Al referred to this columnist as Dumbo. Al did not. The best part is that this columnist thought Al respected him – unaware that to Al, he was Dumbo.

Al loved a phrase from a television commercial. I don't remember the product or service being advertised, but I do remember the commercial, in which someone says sweetly and encouragingly to someone who wished to ask a question: "There are no stupid questions." Then, after the person posed the question, the individual who had said there are no stupid questions said: "That *was* a stupid question."

Al loved that commercial – or, more precisely, Al loved that phrase and he quoted it all the time. "That *was* a stupid question," Al would say of something someone on staff asked, mimicking the precise tone of the person who uttered it in the ad, and he would giggle. Yes, Al giggled.

AL USED COLORFUL LANGUAGE TO convey many different messages, including how much he cared for his employees and their families.

On one occasion, my husband ran into Al in a stadium concourse shortly after we had beaten the Jets in a wild, thrilling game (okay, every victory over the Jets was thrilling). When my husband congratulated Al he looked at my husband and said, "Aw fuck, you're part of this."

When my husband later shared that with me, I melted. Only Al could include "aw fuck" when conveying this a wonderful, special message that my husband was part of the Raiders family.

He again used *fuck* in a heartwarming way after our home was burglarized.

It happened on a Friday, shortly before we were to leave for Kansas City. I let someone in the organization know about the burglary, and that I would fly to Kansas City on Saturday for the game Sunday.

We beat the Chiefs in a thrilling game (okay, all victories over the Chiefs were thrilling).

An hour or so into the flight home, Al asked me where my husband was, and I explained that he was headed to a business meeting in another state. Al responded quite emphatically, "We're not letting you go home to that house alone."

So, someone had told Al about the break-in, I realized. I responded that while I appreciated his concern, I would be fine. He was having none of that. He kept insisting that he'd get me a hotel room. We went back and forth and I finally explained that I wouldn't leave our cat.

"I'll get the cat a hotel room too," he immediately insisted, and he would have. I have no doubt whatsoever that he would have gotten the cat a hotel room too. In fact, he volunteered that he would have someone drive to the house, pick up the cat, and bring it to the hotel. Al Davis, the man who fought bitterly with the NFL, fought for everything he believed in, stood up for the courage of his convictions, who was a tough combatant and a dominating man, was insistent that he would get the cat its own hotel room (and have the cat chauffeured to it), so that I would not go home alone.

Finally, he dropped it. About fifteen minutes later, his wife, who had been reading, looked up at Al and said, "We're not letting Amy go home alone, are we?"

Al responded, in a booming voice heard throughout the area of the plane in which we were seated, "She's not leaving the fuckin' cat."

WORKING ON TRANSACTIONS WITH AL taught me both how to negotiate and how not to negotiate. I learned over the course of my career both how I wished to conduct myself in business and how I did not wish to conduct myself, whether in negotiations or otherwise. I learned what was comfortable for me, and what was not. I learned what I believed was reasonable and acceptable and what I did not believe was reasonable or acceptable. (By the way, it always drove me nuts that Al pronounced negotiate, "ne-go-see-ate" and that he pronounced negotiations, "ne-go-see-ations." I don't know why that drove me nuts, but it did.)

During the course of the first transaction in which I was involved, Al instructed me to contact the owner of the business with which we were negotiating and request – no, it really wasn't a request, it was more of a demand – an additional ten million dollars in consideration. That was a very significant sum at that time and in the context of that transaction. I was so nervous, I asked a coworker to sit with me while I placed the call – I needed moral support.

Throughout my years with the organization, Al was involved in almost every negotiation and transaction of critical importance to the organization, albeit behind the scenes. It struck me at some point fairly early in my career that Al considered those of us who negotiated for him as chess pieces to be deployed, maneuvered, and directed as he wished. I shared that observation with a coworker and he wholeheartedly agreed. I also shared that observation with Al, who responded that he often wished that I was like a chess piece so that he could move me at will, as he wished. Initially, I thought he was kidding. I soon realized that he was not.

As I grew and learned, I realized that I did not share Al's philosophy as to how to negotiate and as to how to reach agreement with others. From time to time, I raised the issue of our differing philosophies and suggested to Al that in our negotiations, we strive to accomplish that which was important to us and concede that which was not, but which was important to the other party or parties to the negotiations. I shared with him my view that it was at best a waste of time and often counterproductive to argue about or demand concessions on issues that were unimportant to us, as so doing could delay or thwart a deal. I also shared with him that someone once told me that the best deals are when each party to an agreement walks away from a negotiation believing that it didn't get all that it wanted.

Once, when a few of us were gathered at the conference table in Al's office discussing a particularly crucial transaction and the state of the negotiations, Al announced that I needed to negotiate like the Russians. He went on to tell me and the assembled group that I must loudly, boldly, forcefully, and emphatically respond "nyet, nyet, nyet" when addressing terms with which we would not agree. He then demonstrated how I must slam my hand on the table when declaring "nyet, nyet, nyet." Al's admiration for this negotiating style and his desire that I employ it had been a topic of discussion and disagreement over the years. He was emphatic and detailed in his instruction and demonstration: "Trask, you have to hit the table with your hand and say, 'nyet, nyet, nyet.'" Al then again recounted the history of the Cuban Missile Crisis and Nikita Khrushchev's role in it and made it clear that he admired Khrushchev's negotiating style. One of my coworkers waited until after Al finished this history lesson and then reminded him that for all their posturing and bombast during the Cuban Missile Crisis, the Russians ultimately turned their boats around. Al looked at him, thought about that for a moment and agreed: "That's right." Then he looked back to me and again instructed me to forcefully declare "nyet, nyet, nyet" while hitting the table with my hand.

At another juncture in this negotiation, Al instructed me to call someone with whom we were negotiating and "tell him he's a cocksucker." "You call him and tell him he's a cocksucker," Al bellowed. I responded by explaining as calmly as I could that calling the person with whom we were negotiating a "cocksucker" was not likely to advance the negotiations or increase the chances of reaching a deal. Al shouted at me: "you call him and tell him he's a cocksucker." Initially, I simply ignored this instruction. But Al didn't drop it – he called me several times a day for a more than a week, asking me if I had yet called this man and told him he was a "cocksucker." I told him that I had not. He was infuriated and again instructed me to do so. So, I tried a different tactic – I said to Al: "Okay, but help me out – is 'cocksucker' one word or two – and if it is two words, 'cock' and 'sucker,' do I place the emphasis on the first or second word." He became so enraged with me – as angry as he had ever been – that I wondered what he might do. But he let it go. I never did call this man a "cocksucker," one word or two. I told Al that I never did. We didn't do a deal with this man – we did a better deal, with someone else. Al and I never spoke of the "call him a cocksucker" incident. It was a sensitive subject.

2

BEHAVIOR PROBLEM

MY FIRST ROAD TRIP WITH THE RAIDERS WAS IN 1990. THAT WAS a big deal, I was told, as it was the first time that a woman – other than a wife who joined her husband on road trips – had traveled with the team to a game. I was determined not to screw this up – not for myself or for anyone else.

Teams hate what they label "distractions." *How could I be a distraction if no one knew I was there*, I thought. I made a commitment to myself that I was going to keep the lowest profile imaginable. I was going to be so low profile that no one would even know I was there.

As part of my low-profile plan, I decided that I wouldn't take one of the chartered buses from our facility to the airport. Instead, I would find a ride and arrive at the airport early. I'd sit in a corner of the boarding area, away from everyone else. Then, once on the plane, I'd sit down, pull out a magazine, shove it in front of my entire face, and stay that way the whole flight. No one would know I was on that plane.

My "low-profile plan" hit a bit of a snag when I arrived at the airport and the underwire in my bra set off a detector. As my bra caused the detector to ping, I turned and saw the first busload of players and coaches heading up the escalator and the stairs towards security. I pleaded with airport officials: "Do whatever you have to do, pat me down, unhook my bra, take it off. Do what you want but let me through before everyone sees what's going on." My pleading didn't work. The players and coaches caught up to me and after a bit of an awkward moment, we all laughed.

Once through security and the boarding area, I again implemented my "low-profile plan."

My strategy upon landing was to board one of the buses waiting for us on the tarmac and to sit by myself, quietly, during the ride to the hotel. Once there, I planned to go directly to my room, and to stay there until game day. Low profile.

So, I got to my room and ordered room service. When I learned that it would take a while for the food to arrive, I decided to take a bubble bath. I was so prepared to hibernate from Friday night to Sunday that I'd packed my own bubbles.

Just as I got out of the tub, there were three really loud knocks on the door. BAM – BAM – BAM.

I remember thinking, *Wow, room service is really early.* I hadn't even had a chance to put on clothes. I was wrapped in a towel with another towel wrapped as a turban around my head.

That knock was loud, I thought as I started moving toward the door. Just then, before I could reach it, the door flew open and Coach Brown shouted "BED CHECK" as a hotel security official stood behind him.

I stood at full attention – in my towel, with my turban, like an absolute dork – and said: "Yes, sir, Mr. Brown, I'm here, in my room, Mr. Brown." I all but saluted.

Coach Brown was, of course, Willie Brown, a great former Raider, one of the best cornerbacks of all time, and a member of the Pro Football Hall of Fame. In Super Bowl XI, Willie intercepted a Fran Tarkenton pass. NFL Films captured that moment – during which the Raiders' radio play-by-play announcer roars "Old Man Willie Brown" as Willie returns that interception 75 yards for a touchdown – and it remains one of the great moments in league history. Whenever I introduced Willie publically or felt like teasing him a bit, I'd refer to him as Old Man Willie Brown. He feigned annoyance, but he I always knew that he loved it.

The moment he left, I called my husband. I was thrilled and excited and proud. I had to share this moment with him. When he answered, I yelled, "I'm part of the team! I got bed checked! I've been accepted! I'm really part of the team!"

"That doesn't sound right," my husband said.

"Oh yes, yes, it means I'm part of the team," I said. I was sincerely thrilled.

"That doesn't sound right," he repeated, adding, "lock the door."

It was many years later that I learned that after he banged on my door, burst in, shouted bed check and then left with the security guard in tow, Willie was laughing so hard at his prank that he had to stop and lean against the wall in the hallway to keep from falling over.

It wasn't a bed check; it was my rookie welcome. Not only was Willie not bothered that I was "a girl," he was comfortable enough that he played a prank on me, including me in a rookie tradition. I know this because Willie and I discussed and laughed about this for decades. Our only disagreement: to this day, when Willie tells the story, he says I was naked. I was not, I was wrapped in a towel.

That lighthearted, silly disagreement (about whether I was wrapped in a towel or not – and I was) aside, there wasn't a moment during my time with the Raiders in which I sensed that Willie was at all concerned with my gender. Our discussions of press coverage, corner blitzes, bump-and-run, single high safety, defensive back hip technique, jamming a receiver, upcoming opponents, player personnel, tendencies, and wins and losses were all without consideration of my gender. Willie Brown is now in his mid 70s – it was a tremendous paradigm shift for him to work with a female colleague – but it didn't bother him.

While Willie was never bothered by my gender, I understood that others may have been. I just didn't care. Why waste my time or energy worrying about my gender or whether it bothered others? Others could waste their time and energy, not me.

I AGAIN FAILED AT MY planned low-profile approach to team travel on another trip later that season. We landed in Denver and sat on the tarmac for what seemed to me to be an interminable amount of time. Because we were on a charter, most people stood up and started walking toward the plane doors well before it taxied to a halt. So, by the time we had stopped on the area of the tarmac on which the buses were waiting, the aisles were packed. Well, we stood and we stood, and we stood. I was close to the plane door, which was open. I edged my way past a few people and squished right up to the door, leaned over, and looked down. I could see the ground, I could see our buses, I could see our advance man speaking with airport personnel – but there were no stairs pulled up to the plane or anywhere near it.

"GET US OFF THIS PLANE," I shouted. After a few moments had elapsed, I again shouted: "FIND SOME STAIRS AND GET US OFF THIS PLANE." I don't have a dainty voice – I speak too loudly as a general rule – and in this instance I was shouting very loudly in order to be heard over all of the airplane and airport noise. I didn't realize how loudly I was shouting until the stairs arrived and we started moving and I heard people talking and laughing about how loud and forceful I was in my directives. I heard Al say, "She got it done."

She got it done.

I subsequently learned that I had angered and offended our advance man, whose job it was to arrange all team travel, by inserting myself into what he (and others) considered his domain and "none of my business" and by being so brash and so loud. But my unabashed willingness to insert myself and my bold, brash manner had had resonated with Al. *She got it done.*

My booming directive to "get us off this plane" was entirely instinctive on my part – I didn't think it through before I acted. This wasn't a calculated decision, designed to assert or insert myself or to send any sort of a message – it was, quite simply, me being me, for better or for worse. In this case, me being me was *both* for better and for worse. In retrospect,

I realized that while this incident suggested to Al that I would not be hesitant to involve myself in an effort to help solve problems, it offended and alienated many of my coworkers, all of whom had been with the organization for far longer than I and most of whom were put off by my commandeering the situation. Players, though, told me that they were impressed.

Not long after I started traveling with the team, I abandoned my attempts at my low-profile plan. As a general rule, I'm not so good at a low-profile approach to life and it wasn't working, anyway.

I figured out that team charters offered a terrific opportunity to interact with players and other coworkers with whom I didn't work on a daily basis. Sometimes, we used the hours on the plane to conduct business. Other times, we simply chatted while congregating in the galleys and aisles.

At one point well into my career, on a trip to Philadelphia, I found myself in the galley with quarterback Rich Gannon, who, unprompted, offered me some worldly advice: how not to order a Philadelphia cheesesteak. I listened and absorbed all of the coaching Rich offered. "Amy," he began, "don't order like you're you, don't say 'none of this, none of that,' or 'extra this, extra that.'" Rich's impression of me was as accurate as it was hilarious. He had perfectly mimicked the precise manner in which I order food.

Rich went on to explain that I should walk up to the vendor and, as would someone from Philadelphia, say only: "Yo, load the bitch up."

The next day, I was out in Philadelphia with two others on staff, saw a cheesesteak vendor, and decided to buy them snacks. With Rich's advice in mind, I strode up to the vendor and said: "Yo, load it up, bitch." Oops. I had never seen my two coworkers move as quickly as they did when they saw the look on the face of the man I had called "bitch."

IN KINDERGARTEN, I WAS LABELED a behavior problem and the label stuck through high school. I didn't listen, I talked when I was not supposed to, I talked back to teachers and other adults, and I misbehaved (or so they said). Many would say this label is still appropriate.

There were times I was sent to stand in the corner just after we said the Pledge of Allegiance and required to remain standing there until class ended. I spent so many hours during kindergarten and elementary school standing in the corner, that I have often marveled that I'm not cross-eyed. Being forced to stand in the corner and then, in higher grades, being kicked out of the classroom to stand outside, went on for many years.

I was not a good student, I was told. I was a problem, they added.

I remember my sixth-grade teacher summoning my mother to school to meet with him. I also remember that I recognized at the time that this was not a good thing. He told my mother that he was aware that my older siblings were very smart, but that I was not and that I was not destined to go to college. I was in the sixth grade – college was a long way off – but he was convinced that I wouldn't get in. He informed my mother that she needed to have entirely different expectations for me than she did for my siblings and that trade school was the only realistic expectation for me. There is nothing whatsoever wrong with attending – or aspiring to attend – trade school, of course; nothing at all. But elementary school is not the time for someone to make any determination or reach any conclusion about any child.

I was standing in the hallway outside the classroom – but the transoms (that's what they were called – transoms) were open – and I overheard the entire conversation, including my mother's response, the sum and substance of which I remember to this day. Her voice was controlled, but I knew she was angry. No one, she explained to this teacher, should ever label any child. No one, she added, should ever preconceive what any child is capable of achieving. She told him that as an educator, he should know better.

Perhaps because I was labeled a behavior problem in kindergarten or perhaps because from the time I can remember, my mother expressed her disdain for labeling people, I have always abhorred them.

Labels are a cheap, lazy convenience.

Labels are often attached to players. One label I abhor as much or more than any is "thug." That label is not only offensive for the simple fact that it is a label; it is offensive because it is insidious.

I periodically share my strongly held views about the use of this label. Toward the conclusion of the 2013 season, Richard Sherman was labeled a thug by many. As I said then and as I have repeated many times since, if Richard Sherman is considered a thug, then I am proud to call myself a thug, too. Each time I have said this, people have playfully responded that there are some in league circles who may, in fact, consider me a thug. Well even if that is true, that's fine; I will proudly stand (as a pearl-wearing) thug alongside many others who have been labeled as such.

I do think that that being labeled a behavior problem – or, actually being a behavior problem – is one of the reasons I fell in love with the Raiders.

While I was a student at Cal, the Raiders were still in Oakland and I attended a few games. Something about the Raiders resonated with me – the players were branded renegades, outlaws, and criminals. The owner gave second (and third and fourth) chances to those who wouldn't get a chance on any other team. The owner didn't seem to care whether a player had been labeled (or was) a behavior problem. The owner didn't seem to care about labels at all. Raiders players were zany and different.

What better team for someone who had been branded a behavior problem in kindergarten to pick as her football team?

The Raiders moved to Los Angeles the same year I graduated from Cal and moved back to Los Angeles to attend graduate school. (Actually, the organization had tried to move two years earlier, but was ordered back to Oakland by the court.) I attended a few games while in graduate school, as I had while in college. In fact, one of my earliest dates with my husband was to a game in the Coliseum – we purchased the only seats we could afford, smack dab in what was referred to as the "peristyle end zone" (the end zone that was about a hundred miles from the field).

JUST AS I WASN'T A particularly good student in elementary school, I wasn't a particularly good student in junior high school. By my family's standards, I was a crummy student. I didn't do homework. I didn't even bring my books home from school; I left them in my locker. I didn't do well on tests – really, very poorly, by my parents' standards – and I received what my parents considered very disappointing grades. I just didn't care about school. I was able to get by without doing anything, and I had no desire to do more than that.

And then, in my first year of high school, came a magnificent teacher who changed the trajectory of my life. That's not an overstatement; she really did. Her name was Jeanne Hernandez and she was my 10th-grade English teacher. One day during the first month of high school, Mrs. Hernandez, disgusted by yet another of my obnoxious responses to a question and my obnoxious, disinterested attitude in general, pointed a finger directly at me (it looked to me like a talon) and motioned to the door. It was clear that she was directing me to leave the room, which I did. She walked out with me and as we stood on the outdoor walkway that ran in front of all of the classrooms in that area, she told me that she was not going to stand for my attitude or my behavior, that she expected more of me, and that she would not accept less than she believed that I could achieve. That was it. Discussion over. I was stunned and initially, I was angry. But then I realized that I also felt good. Mrs. Hernandez saw reason to challenge me – she was going to demand more of me than I had ever demanded of myself – she cared. That was the first time I didn't talk back or mouth off in school. Mrs. Hernandez walked back into the classroom, as did I.

It is said that a teacher can change a child's life and Mrs. Hernandez changed mine. From that day forward, I paid attention, I tried, I believed that I could do better, and I did do better. Because of her, I got better grades and I went to college.

A number of years after I began working for the Raiders, I wrote a letter to Mrs. Hernandez and sent it to the then-principal of the high school I attended, with a note asking him to forward it to her. I don't know if she ever received that letter, but I hope she did. In my letter, I explained that she changed my life – that she altered its course – and I thanked her.

3
GET THE COFFEE

I ATTENDED MY FIRST LEAGUE MEETING NOT LONG AFTER JOINING the organization on a full-time basis. This meeting was what the league refers to as a "two-per-club meeting" and as the name suggests, clubs were allowed to be represented by no more than two attendees. In most cases, the controlling owner typically represented his club and brought with him someone he designated to also represent the club.

I was told that my attendance at that meeting marked the first time a woman unrelated to ownership had ever represented a club at, or even attended, a league meeting. I don't know if that was the case. I also don't care. When I was told that I was the first female executive to attend a league meeting, I accepted that it was true but I gave it no thought. Al Davis asked me to attend the meeting – and to represent the Raiders – and that was what mattered to me.

We checked into the hotel the night before the meeting. Before we walked away from the hotel front desk, Al turned to me and said, "Get the chairs."

I was not surprised or confused by this statement; I knew to expect it. I knew what he meant and I knew what I had to do. I had been told by Jeff Birren, the organization's senior lawyer who later became its general counsel (and the person who took me on as an intern), that it was imperative that I "get the chairs," which Jeff explained meant the precise chairs in the precise location Al expected. Getting the chairs was not just a big deal for the Raiders; it was a big deal for all clubs.

Over the years, each club had staked out for itself a certain spot in the meeting room and well before each meeting started, a representative from each club secured the chairs associated with those spots. It was as if the spots had been assigned – but they had not been, they had been claimed. Frankly, it would have been a lot easier if the chairs were assigned.

I had been told which chairs Al wanted – no, which chairs he expected. I was focused. I was not going to screw this up. I would get the right chairs, even if I had to sleep in the hallway outside the meeting room to do so.

The next morning, having secured our chairs the night before, I arrived at the meeting room before the meeting was scheduled to begin. As I walked in, I saw a large group in the back of the room, enjoying coffee and conversing, so I walked to that area and joined the group. Almost immediately, the owner of another team asked me to get him coffee.

It took a moment for his request to sink in. When it did, I looked around the room and realized that I was the only woman there who was not part of the hotel catering staff. This man must have assumed I was part of that staff. I smiled, asked him how he'd like his coffee, and got it for him. I could have refused to do so. I could have admonished him for asking the question. Instead, I quickly decided that I would have some fun at his expense. I was delighted with the prospect that when the meeting was called to order in a matter of moments, he would realize that I did not leave the room with the hotel staff but, rather, took a seat with the other club executives and owners. I thought that would be a very funny, effective way to make a point. It certainly amused me.

This owner was in his sixties or seventies, I think. He took his coffee with a bit of cream. He thanked me, but he did not tip me.

When the meeting was called to order, I followed Al to our seats. The seats I'd staked out the night before.

As we walked to our seats, the room became very quiet and I was able to hear some of the comments. Some people were using hushed tones; others were speaking conversationally.

Is she staying in the room? Looks like she's with Al. Is she coming to the meeting? I think she's coming to the meeting. Figures it would be Al. She's not leaving. Who is she? Why is she here?

I was later told by quite a few people in and around the league that many people begrudged Al for bringing a woman into that room. I suspect that many of the men who resented Al for bringing a woman into that room were the same men who resented him for being the first to hire a Latino head coach and later the first African American head coach of the modern era.

As for the owner who asked me to fetch him coffee, we became good friends, and he emerged as one of my staunchest supporters. He had no issue with my gender. He was simply surprised. The rules of the game had changed during his tenure as an owner – indeed, during his lifetime. And yes, he was mortified that he had asked me to fetch him coffee. And yes, handing this in the manner I did was effective. We laughed for decades about this and I periodically asked him if he wanted coffee, just to annoy him – and I reminded him that he should have tipped me.

IT WASN'T UNTIL MANY YEARS after I joined the league that it began considering the issue of diversity and inclusiveness. *Welcome to the party*, I thought.

I remember participating on a conference call arranged for the 32 member clubs to discuss a proposed rule that would ultimately become known as the Rooney Rule. At the conclusion of the league presentation, each club representative was asked to express his (or in my case her) thoughts and ask questions. When it was my turn, I shared my thoughts on the proposed rule and then noted that Al had hired without regard to race, ethnicity, religion, or gender for decades; that neither the league office nor any other club had our decades-long record for diversity and inclusiveness; and that Al had never needed a rule to mandate doing the right thing. I understood that this would not be well received – but it was true. I also suggested that the rule really should be called the Al Davis Rule. That was snotty.

When I told Al that I had suggested the rule be named for him, he got annoyed and told me emphatically he wasn't interested in having a rule named for him.

To be clear: of course we supported diversity and inclusiveness, and if it took a rule to get other clubs to do the right thing, so be it. I just wanted it known that we didn't need a rule to do the right thing. Also to be clear, I don't begrudge the fact that the rule is named after Dan Rooney, a man I respect and who encouraged me throughout my career; I simply wanted to make the point that Al had done this for decades.

In its effort to address diversity and inclusiveness, the league at some point started including a session on this topic at most league meetings. It struck me that Raiders representatives should not have to sit through these presentations, so each time one of those sessions was about to start at a meeting at which Al was present, I turned to him and asked in a loud and childish manner, "Why do we have to sit through this? Why can't we go to the gym?" My point was, of course, that he was the last person who needed to sit through these lessons. Each time I did this, Al told me to be quiet.

Many years after the adoption of the Rooney Rule, the league announced that it would expand the rule (or enact a similar one) to encompass women. Although I was no longer in the league when this occurred, I again suggested that the rule be named the Al Davis Rule. Were Al alive, he would have again been annoyed with my suggestion and he would have again told me emphatically that he didn't want a rule named after him.

AS I REFLECT ON MOMENTS in which I was childish, I realize how tolerant Al was of this occasional behavior. It amused him at times, it annoyed him at times, but he allowed me to be me. He was more tolerant than anyone would have imagined he would be. He was more tolerant than I would, or should, have expected him to be. I learned a lot about life from Al. He taught me many things, some of with which I agreed with, some of with which I did not. Just as Al was always himself, he permitted me to be myself – for good and for bad. He allowed me to grow up on the job. He allowed me to grow up while a Raider.

WHEN I JOINED THE ORGANIZATION and subsequently began attending league meetings, the Raiders and the NFL were engaged in a longstanding dispute. The issue underlying the dispute, which began while I was still in college, was franchise relocation. In essence, Al wanted to move his team, the league tried to prohibit him from so doing, he did so anyway, and litigation ensued. That litigation lasted years and created tremendous enmity between Al and the league office, and between Al and almost all other club owners.

The vast majority of owners were livid with Al about the dispute, the resultant litigation and Al's ardent refusal to engage in what they referred to as a "league first" approach. I recall listening to many owners admonish Al for his actions and for thinking only of his organization and not of the league as a whole. Of course, I thought when hearing this, it was easier to think of the league first and the league as a whole when one was treated well by the league office. We were not always treated well by the league office. Were we not treated well by the league office because Al was combative? Or was Al combative because we were not treated well? I don't know the answer, as both the league's disparate treatment of the Raiders and Al's combative posture with the league predated me. My impression, though, was that it was a bit of both. In scientific terms, it was a feedback loop.

SOME OF THE OWNERS WHO were the angriest with Al were among the longest-tenured and respected owners. Yet, notwithstanding that these men had deep philosophical and business differences with Al, they were remarkably welcoming to me.

Lamar Hunt of the Kansas City Chiefs was the owner who offered me the greatest encouragement when I joined the league and for decades thereafter. Lamar vehemently disagreed with Al's position on relocation as well as with Al's method of doing business. Lamar certainly had no reason to extend himself or to go to the lengths he did to make me feel welcome in the league, but from the first time we met until the last time we interacted, he encouraged me. I will always have a deep and heartfelt appreciation for the support he offered me at a time he had every reason not to. Lamar's wife, Norma, and his sons, Clark and Daniel, were equally gracious. No matter the intensity of the conflict between the Raiders and the league, they were kind and encouraging. The Hunt family represents the very best of the league.

Whenever I share my thoughts about the Hunts, people remark that it's odd that a Raider speaks so glowingly of a Chief – or in this case Chiefs, plural. No, it's not odd. While clubs want nothing more than to beat one another on game day, they work with one another on many other days, and in many ways. On game days, I visited with the owner and employees of the club we were to play. Prior to kickoff, we exchanged warm greetings, talked about league matters and then, laughingly, wished one another a miserable game. We wished one another the worst in terms of the outcome, but we expressed hope for an injury-free game. I wanted to win each game more than I wanted anything, but I never wanted an athlete on either team to suffer an injury.

Ralph Wilson of the Buffalo Bills was another league stalwart who welcomed me. Like Lamar, Ralph had a relationship with Al that dated back to their years in the American Football League. The AFL was a direct competitor of the NFL until the two leagues merged in 1970. Some of the owners who ran that league, like Al, Lamar, and Ralph, together battled the NFL until the merger. These three great owners were unified as AFL owners but years later, in the NFL, Lamar and Ralph opposed Al on many league matters and he opposed them. Like Lamar, Ralph nevertheless encouraged me throughout my career.

Many years into my career, during a contentious negotiation with the players, Ralph was at odds with the league and the majority of the clubs. He was forthright and firm when articulating his disagreement on the floor of the league meetings and he took tremendous heat for that. At one point, as he sat down after speaking, I whispered to him that I admired how he stood strong in the pocket in the face of tremendous pressure, and in response he asked if I would block for him. I told him that it would be my honor to do so. From that day forward – until the last time I saw him – Ralph always said to me, "I'm still standing in the pocket, are you still blocking for me?" I assured him that I was and that I always would.

The Steelers' Dan Rooney and the Giants' Wellington Mara, two other legendary owners who were diametrically opposed to Al's business practices and legal positions, were also welcoming and encouraging.

Lamar was inducted into three Halls of Fame including the NFL's. Ralph was the third-longest-tenured owner in NFL history and is also in the Hall of Fame. Dan was inducted into the Hall of Fame in 2000. Wellington is in the Hall of Fame after winning two Super Bowls.

I found it interesting four owners who were among the longest-tenured were the first to welcome me. These men provided encouragement throughout my time in the league.

We didn't make it easy for these men to welcome or to encourage me, but they did.

Tom Benson of the New Orleans Saints, a very influential owner who for many years served as the chairman of the league's powerful finance committee, also welcomed and encouraged me. There wasn't a meeting I attended for over a decade in which he didn't vehemently express his anger at Al, more so than did any other owner. And yet, at one point during a break in one of those meetings, Tom pulled me aside and shared with me a very meaningful comment: he told me that he thought it tremendously beneficial for the Raiders and thus the league as a whole that Al added me to the organization.

Pat Bowlen of the Denver Broncos was also outspoken about his disdain for Al's business positions and practices, yet when he realized that I wished to resolve the lawsuits between the league and the Raiders, he was the first to offer me assistance.

Mike Brown of the Cincinnati Bengals is another owner who helped me. Like Al, Mike maintained and articulated positions adverse to the league and he thus understood the difficulty of so doing. When I did so on behalf of the Raiders, Mike always made a point of letting me know that he understood how difficult it was to do so and I appreciated that he did.

I share all this because I know that when I first walked into that league owners' sanctuary, these men were surprised. After all, this was new — a woman unrelated to ownership was now behind those closed meeting room doors and representing a club.

THROUGHOUT THE ERA IN WHICH those disputes roared, we took positions and made statements at league meetings with which I strongly disagreed. While I shared my disagreement with Al in the privacy of our offices, once at the meetings we presented our positions as those of the organization, as a united front. During this period, we also abstained when matters were voted upon by club owners. The practice of abstaining also predated my time with the organization. Initially, the organization abstained for legal reasons. Thereafter, the organization also abstained at times because Al believed the matter proposed was, to use the word he did, ludicrous. Al liked that word and he used it often, in a variety of contexts.

I joked for years that were we (Raiders employees) to play word bingo with Al's favorite expressions, the person with "aw fuck" and "ludicrous" would be Al Bingo champion.

When I began attending meetings with Al, he abstained on the club's behalf when matters were put to a vote. Later, I did so on behalf of the organization. This certainly didn't endear me to anyone in the room. That our abstentions were a source of consternation was made clear to me. Every time we headed to a break after a vote from which I had abstained, at least one president or chief executive representing another team would criticize or mock me about our abstention.

Ultimately, I ended the tradition of abstaining and voted yes or no on all matters put to a vote. League officials and club owners were then annoyed in instances I voted no, as they always wanted unanimous affirmation of proposals. I would ask – in an ever-so-sweet, teasing tone of voice – whether they missed the day and age in which the Raiders would abstain and whether they would prefer that we would revert to that, rather than voting no. I stopped the practice of abstaining many years before I resigned, but our reputation for abstaining stayed with us.

EVEN WHILE IN THE MIDST of the disagreements and hostilities, the Raiders and the league cooperated on a wide variety of business matters. League office employees contacted me on a regular basis and we worked on all sorts of things. On those occasions on which they asked me to do something that would benefit the league as a whole, but which was to the detriment of the Raiders, they acknowledged that they understood how difficult this would be. In one instance, league officials contacted me and requested that we drop a claim in a pending player grievance. The problem, they explained, was that the position we had advanced in our defense could result in a decision that might be harmful to all clubs. The league executives who contacted me acknowledged that they understood that I did not work on player contracts or grievances, but explained that they needed my help. They went on to explain that they understood that Al would have to agree to any change in our position and that they believed that I was the only one they could turn to who would try to, and perhaps could, convince him to do so. So, while it appeared to the public that the league and the Raiders were at odds, we found ways to work together on many league matters.

A sensational league executive with whom I worked on a regular basis once told me that he appreciated that we were able to "disagree without being disagreeable." I thought that was a terrific manner in which to articulate a terrific goal. Reasonable minds can differ and I tried, when disagreeing, to do so agreeably. For the most part I succeeded, but not always. I improved as I matured.

I often analogized working closely with league officials on some matters, while we were battling on others, to the working relationship between two cartoon characters: Ralph E. Wolf and Sam Sheepdog. While Ralph and Sam battled fiercely over matters about which they disagreed (to wit: the sheep), they were friendly and collegial when not involved in a heated dispute (over the sheep). I shared this analogy with some league executives and after a bit of thought, they concurred. Whenever a particular league executive contacted me about league business, he asked, "Am I Ralph or Sam this time?"

Of course, not all interactions with club owners were as pleasant or invigorating as the ones previously mentioned. There was the instance at a league meeting in which a club owner stood up to respond to something I said and began his remarks with "Listen, girlie." He actually said, "Listen, girlie." The only other time I had heard someone use the word "girlie" was when I was a preteen and my grandma shouted, "Hey girlie!" from the car to a teenager on the street to get her attention. I was so mortified that I slid down to the floor of the car to hide.

Al wasn't at this meeting but I believe that had he been, he would have had a terrific response. I don't know, though, whether this owner would have called me girlie had Al been in attendance.

When this owner called me girlie, most everyone in the room looked at me to see how I would respond, while some averted their eyes. My immediate and natural reaction was to laugh loudly. A grown man, in a business meeting, in the then-20th century, referred to a female executive as girlie. And so I laughed, loudly.

A number of people I respect have suggested that I should have denounced him for his absurd comment. I think erupting in loud, spontaneous laughter and treating him dismissively in front of league officials and other club owners was an effective response. I know that I much prefer being yelled at to being dismissed or ignored.

AT ONE TWO-PER-CLUB LEAGUE MEETING, two club executives – Steve Gutman of the New York Jets and Carmen Policy of the San Francisco 49ers – engaged in what became a heated argument on the floor of the meeting room. They were standing fairly close to and were shouting at one another. During the argument one man pointed at the other and said, "You, sir, are alarmingly disingenuous."

Jack Donlan, the executive representing the Tampa Bay Buccaneers at the meeting, was seated immediately beside me. Upon hearing that remark, he swiveled in his chair to face me and said, "I hear you're supposed to be pretty smart, so tell me, is calling someone alarmingly disingenuous the same thing as calling him a fucking liar?" Only, he had a thick Boston accent, so "fucking liar" sounded like "fuckin' lyah."

Well, I began explaining – quite precisely – that yes, calling someone alarmingly disingenuous is the same thing as calling someone a fucking liar, because if one wanted to simply call someone a liar – not a fucking liar – one would say he was being disingenuous, not alarmingly disingenuous.

At that point, Al – who was seated behind me as we faced the front of the room – poked me in the back and said, "He didn't ask for a fuckin' grammar lesson." Oh.

AT ANOTHER TWO-PER-CLUB MEETING I attended without Al, a club representative made an assertion – a representation – about the Raiders that was patently untrue.

As he was speaking, I did what attendees did when they wished to be heard and walked to the standing microphone nearest me, to wait my turn to speak. After this representative concluded his remarks, I began speaking. Just as I started to speak, then-commissioner Paul Tagliabue interrupted me and stated bluntly and dismissively, and in a manner suggesting that it was not open for dispute, that we needed to move on. He expected me to sit down, as did everyone else in the room. It never occurred to me to sit down, so I didn't move. I stayed at the microphone and said, "No, I have something to say." The room was silent. I remained standing where I was for what seemed like many moments as the silence continued. Finally, after a long pause, the commissioner said curtly, "Make it quick."

It didn't strike me at the time that I had done anything odd or out of the ordinary. My refusal to acquiesce to the commissioner's direction and to sit down was not a political statement, it was not a form of protest. I had something to say and although I was told that I should sit down, I wanted to say it. I considered it my responsibility to represent the organization and I intended to do that to the best of my ability. I believed that to do so, I had to respond to the misrepresentations that were made. So, no, it didn't strike me as odd – it struck me as appropriate. Apparently, it struck everyone else in the room as inappropriate and it struck many as offensive.

As we went to a break a bit later, one club owner walked by me as he was exiting the room, and without slowing his pace, he leaned in, ever so slightly, and whispered: "You popped my buttons." He subsequently called Al and told him the same thing. I'd never before heard that expression and I didn't know whether he intended it as a compliment or an insult.

It didn't occur to me when the commissioner interrupted and tried to silence me that he did so because I was a woman. I am confident that he would have acted in precisely the same manner had I been male. It also didn't occur to me that those who were offended by my refusal to yield to the commissioner were offended because I was a woman. They were offended because I didn't defer to the authority of the commissioner, as others did. I believe that they would also have been offended by my action had I been a man.

Many people I respect have criticized me for not thinking the commissioner's effort to silence me was gender based and for not responding accordingly. Well, I didn't believe it was gender based, but let's say for a moment that it was, and he acted as he did because I was a woman. Then wasn't my reaction – refusing to follow his directive or to yield to pressure – the most effective response? What would have been better? If I made a speech? I was told to sit down; I refused to do so. I wanted to speak; I spoke. I believe that I did the best thing I could: I did my job.

BUT BACK TO THE TIME I was first instructed to "get the seats."

The seating arrangements, the lengths to which people go to secure seats for their respective clubs, and the methods they employ in so doing could serve as a study in organizational and social behavior. Really, it always reminded me, from the first meeting I attended until the last, of junior high school.

Throughout my career, meeting rooms were set up with three very long tables running from and perpendicular to one long head table. Seated at the head table are the commissioner; senior league executives; and, when circumstances warrant, committee members and other speakers.

Clubs sit on both sides of the long tables, which, as noted, run perpendicular to the head table. At each and every meeting I attended for roughly a quarter of a century, the Raiders sat in the same seats at the same table, as did most every single other club. It was a stressful scramble to make sure one got the seats. Really, I found getting the seats to be more stressful than making substantive presentations or engaging in a debate on the floor of the meeting. As stressful as it was, it taught me a skill. Whenever I enter a crowded coffee place or other location, I am well equipped to "get the seats." Friends and family marvel at what they consider my good fortune. It's not good fortune or luck; I am an experienced seat-getter.

I was not the only club executive who rushed to get into the room the night before each meeting in order to claim desired seats. We all did this. We found a way into the meeting room and scribbled our club names down on the pads of paper set out at each place. We begged security to let us in, we found back doors when security would not let us in the front doors, we did anything we could to get the seats. We helped one another, too. There were groups who worked in concert – we had seat-getting collectives. We shared travel plans with one another to determine who among us would be the first to arrive and we updated one another about travel delays. The first to arrive would scribble not only his or her team name on the pads, but those of the other teams in our little collective.

One time, the operating head of another club that was not yet a part of our collective actually circulated to our group an email with a PDF of his artistic rendering of the tables (with club names noted at our respective seats) attached, and a request that the first of us to arrive secure seats for his club, as he and the owner of the team for which he worked would be arriving at the last minute. Think about that: a very senior executive, the operating head of a club, took the time to make and circulate a PDF with an illustration of the table, with club names noted.

We took this seriously.

On one occasion when I went to get the seats the night before a meeting, I couldn't find a way to access the room from the lobby or any other public area, so I poked around and found a back entrance into a kitchen, which adjoined the meeting room. I then crept through the dark passages in the kitchen to gain access to the room.

The kitchen was dark and creepy. I recall thinking as I crept around that it was like something from a Nancy Drew novel. Once I made it into the meeting room, I scrawled the team names on the pads in front of the seats, and began retracing my steps as quickly as I could, through that dark, quiet, scary, creepy kitchen. I heard noises and I started moving even faster. Now it struck me as something out of a bad horror movie, not simply a Nancy Drew novel. It turned out it was an executive from another club who was doing the same thing. We scared the crap out of each other and laughed at the lengths we went to save seats.

Why have I gone to such lengths to describe the get-the-seat process? Because these are roughly billion-dollar businesses – owned by people worth a lot of money – and their most senior employees (presidents, chief executives, and general managers) expend crazy amounts of time and effort just to get the seats. Each time I did so throughout my career, I thought that fans would find this get-the-seats routine amazing, ridiculous, and perplexing. I sure did. Whenever I describe the efforts that clubs go to just to save seats, people think it's nuts. They're right.

And really, if we all wanted to sit in the same seats for every meeting, why was there a race to get the seats? Why didn't we all just take those same seats for each meeting, without having to stake a claim by writing our club names on the little pads of paper? Because in some instances – particularly meetings in which three people were allowed – some clubs encroached, taking a seat from another club's preferred position. And, when a club changed ownership, sometimes new owners or new club representatives took the "wrong" seats.

Getting the seats wasn't about power or supremacy among clubs, it was about preference and habit and routine. I thought it more silly than anything.

I actually thought that it would be a good idea for owners and executives to sit in a new, rotating location for each meeting to facilitate or compel interaction and dialogue between and among clubs that might otherwise not occur. I thought it could lead to greater understandings and relationships. Al wouldn't have wanted that. He liked our seats.

I suggested on a few occasions that we pass a resolution adopting a seating chart in order to save everyone from having to get into that room late at night, wake up hours early, beg and plead with security, or sneak in through scary kitchens, all in an effort to save our seats. No such resolution ever passed, so I continued to get the seats at meetings.

I wasn't asked to get the seats because of my gender. I would have had to do that no matter my gender. In fact, before I started attending league meetings, other club executives who attended with Al – all men – got the seats. As noted, it was one of those men, Jeff, who explained to me which of the seats were ours, and the importance of securing them for the meeting. Jeff didn't have to do this; he did so because he wanted me to succeed, he wanted me to be my best, and throughout my career he consistently and generously extended himself to help me and many others do so. That's what good teammates do – they help their teammates be the best they can be. I had teammates who helped me be better than I otherwise would have been, and I hope that I helped my teammates be better than they otherwise would have been.

FROM THE FIRST LEAGUE MEETING I attended until the last, I noticed that most owners behaved in a deferential manner, acceding to the commissioner and the league office in almost every way. That struck me as odd. I always wondered why such wealthy, powerful men – men who were titans of business, men who were worth vast sums of money – would be so acquiescent. I don't use the words deferential or acquiescent in a pejorative sense; perhaps cooperative is a better word. But no matter the word, the extent of the deference shown the commissioner and the league office surprised me, even once I understood the reasons for that deference.

There was only one occasion during all of my years in the league on which an owner confronted the commissioner. This owner stood up in a two-per-club meeting, loomed over and pointed at then-commissioner Tagliabue and in a loud, authoritative voice said, "Hey pal, you work for me." As I sat next to Al in our seats all the way on the other side of the room, I started squirming, trying not to jump from my chair and throw my arms overhead in a victory sign, and I was practically cheering. "Calm down," Al said.

This occasion aside, owners were consistently deferential and acquiescent. I eventually concluded that this is because clubs understand the power of the league office. The league office controls scheduling. The league office can and does direct enormous amounts of money (via sponsors, advertisers, or otherwise) to clubs it selects or to effectuate business ends it desires, or both. The league office highlights and promotes preferred clubs in programming and advertising campaigns. The league office can and does dispense or withhold a myriad of favors.

After Hurricane Katrina, when there were rumblings that the Saints were considering moving to San Antonio, the league directed substantial amounts of sponsorship money and advertising resources to the Saints to make it financially palatable for them to remain in New Orleans. Was this wrong? No. I thought it was the right thing to do for many reasons. My point is that the league is able to direct substantial revenues to clubs of its choosing, for any number of reasons, commendable or otherwise.

There was one owner who was never deferential. It was Al.

A SENIOR LEAGUE EXECUTIVE ONCE recounted this story to me: one spring, when the schedule for the upcoming season had been all but finalized and was presented to the commissioner for his ultimate approval, the commissioner was informed the schedule was fair with one exception. The Raiders' schedule, this executive explained to the commissioner, included a disproportionate number of rough patches (back-to-back long-distance road trips and long-distance road trips on short weeks, among other things), considerably more than that of any other team. The commissioner's response: "This schedule is fine, release it."

The commissioner's proclamation may not have signaled that he wanted the Raiders to have – or didn't care if the Raiders had – the worst schedule. The commissioner's decision may have simply reflected his view that the proposed schedule was the best for the league as a whole, that all teams cannot be made happy, or that no team will ever be entirely happy with its schedule. Did it bother him or did he affirmatively like that the team that had the disproportionate amount of rough patches in its schedule was the Raiders? I don't know. I know only that this was called to the commissioner's attention and that he approved the schedule. I wondered if he would have done so had the team with that schedule been owned by one of the more agreeable, deferential owners. I don't know the answer to that, either. I don't, however, believe that he would have approved that schedule if it had been for a team owned by one of the powerful owners.

So Al wasn't deferential, acquiescent, or particularly cooperative. That schedule was approved. Conclude what you'd like.

ON MANY OCCASIONS, AL CAUTIONED me about what he believed to be the tremendous power of the league office. A few times, when we were poised to take a position adverse to the league, when we were in the midst of our disputes with the league, when we defied the league, Al warned me: "The league is powerful, baby, it's powerful. It's the most powerful organization in the world." I recall him musing that he could not think of anyone with more power than the commissioner. "Not anyone?" I asked sarcastically. He gave my question serious and considerable thought, and offered his view that maybe the president of the United States or the pope were as powerful. No, not the pope, he decided, maybe though, the president. Only on rare occasions did Al acknowledge that we needed to expect that such power would be wielded to our detriment.

I know that other club owners were wary of the power of the league office. Over the years I asked a number of them why they voted in favor of a proposed matter when they had shared with me that they were staunchly opposed to it. In response to my question, they referenced that power.

Of course, there are many reasons that owners may defer to the league office. Certainly, owners are fully capable of taking charge and have every right to change league management and policy if and as they wish. After all, and as that one owner noted, the commissioner works (and in fact, all league employees work) for the owners. That they have not done so suggests that they – or at least the owners who are powerful or influential and thus able to effectuate change – are pleased, or at least content, with the status quo.

From the time I started attending league meetings, I observed that there were owners who appeared to hold and to exert more influence than other owners. These owners are appointed to more committees than are less powerful owners and they are appointed to the most significant committees. Thus, it may be that what appears to be deference to the league office by all owners is in fact be deference only by those owners with less power than others. The more powerful owners direct league policy; the less powerful owners acquiesce to it. It was my observation that these owners with less power and influence feared trying to effectuate change, as a failed attempt to do so may have resulted in retaliatory action or unfavorable treatment. Of course, none of this is atypical of many businesses and organizations.

Al was not a powerful owner, but that didn't bother him. He didn't care about fitting in; he wasn't interested in being one of the boys or being part of any sort of inner circle. He wasn't interested in being on league committees and agreed to serve on only one that I can recall, and he did that only for a discrete period of time. Interestingly, Al wasn't bothered that the commissioner appointed me to several committees – it just wasn't something he wished to do.

Al was an iconoclast – not in every way, but in most ways. In other ways, he was quite traditional. Al cannot be easily or breezily described.

A DISCUSSION OF POWER REMINDS me of one of my favorite photographs of Al. It shows him on the sideline before a game shaking hands with Darth Vader.

For this particular game, we had arranged a sponsorship that included as one of its elements Darth's attendance at a game.

I approached Al on the sideline during warmups and asked him to greet Darth.

"Who the fuck is Darth Vader?" Al responded, annoyed that I was asking him to interact with someone pregame.

Al never wished to interact with sponsors, whether on game day or otherwise, and he almost always refused. In this instance, he agreed to walk a few steps and greet Darth, noting in an annoyed tone that he was doing so for me. *Okay*, I thought, *this sponsorship is for the benefit of the organization, but you're greeting Darth Vader for me.*

Al politely extended his hand. The expression on his face was magnificent, as was the gracious greeting he extended to Darth.

Al and Darth Vader – perfect. *If ever there was a meeting that was meant to be, that was it*, I thought.

Also at this game and on the sideline as part of this sponsorship were the Storm Troopers. I was utterly delighted, as were others to whom I eagerly pointed this out, that as the game neared a very exciting end and our fans were cheering us on, the Storm Troopers standing on the sideline were cheering too, arms in the air, waving towels.

I remember thinking, *Even the Storm Troopers are happy.*

AL HAD A LOT OF "fuck you" in him. He didn't back down when he believed he was right or when he was pursuing something he wanted. There were instances in which that led to bad business decisions and bad results. Even when we warned Al that certain actions or inactions would lead to bad results, he was unmovable and unmoved. There were times when that infuriated me, frustrated me, and drove me absolutely crazy.

But that same "fuck you" in Al was part of what made him such a tremendous man. Al had the courage of his convictions. There were circumstances in which sticking to his convictions was the right thing to do – not the easy thing to do, not the popular thing to do – but the right thing to do, and Al had the courage to do it. The "fuck you" in Al made him the man he was.

I have some "fuck you" in me too. I had that "fuck you" in me before I joined the Raiders. It may have been honed while I was with the organization – certainly, the environment wasn't such that I needed to squelch it.

Sometimes, having a bit of "fuck you" in you can be a good thing. I'd rather have it than not.

One might think that because I have some "fuck you" in me, Al would not have tolerated me or that we would not have been able to coexist, let alone work together. I actually think that Al liked that I had some "fuck you" in me and I believe that is why, although we often wanted to strangle one another, he trusted me.

I cared deeply for Al and I know that he cared for me. Our relationship worked.

4

MOM

ABOUT 15 YEARS AFTER I STARTED WORKING FULL-TIME FOR THE Raiders, my mom very casually mentioned that she might be Al's biggest fan. Her statement surprised me and the simple, quiet manner in which she shared it was out of character for her.

I knew this wasn't a statement of appreciation for the vertical passing game or Al's philosophy that the quarterback must go down, and must go down hard. It struck me that it was something more. After all, it was my mom who once said to me after a particularly thrilling victory over the Denver Broncos (okay, all victories over the Broncos were thrilling) that it's too bad that both teams can't win. I was incredulous when she said that and I looked at her like she was nuts. So, when she told me that she might well be Al's biggest fan, I was intrigued.

My mom went to college in the mid 1940s and she majored in chemistry. Toward the end of her senior year of college, quite a few pharmaceutical and other companies came to campus to interview students for entry-level positions for chemists. My mom interviewed with numerous companies but none offered her a job. Finally, at the conclusion of her last interview, she asked the representative of the pharmaceutical company why no one had extended her an offer. "Even my dumb lab partner, who couldn't pass his chemistry labs without my help," my mom told the representative, "got job offers."

My mom shared with me that the representative explained to her in a very matter-of-fact manner that since she was beautiful and had a diamond ring on her left hand, no company would waste its time with her.

My mom never expressed any bitterness about that or any of the challenges she faced. It was my impression that she never thought about them. She went on to earn masters and doctoral degrees and to enjoy a roughly 40-year career. Yeah, that diamond ring really held her back.

It occurred to me that my mom appreciated that Al didn't care that I was a woman, the way those companies had cared about her gender so many years earlier, and that he afforded me the opportunity he did without regard to my gender. I realized that this was the world in which my mom had hoped I would live.

I shared that story with Al. He responded, "Aw fuck," but I noticed what I considered a very special – one might even say sweet - look on his face when he said that.

I miss hearing Al say, "Aw fuck."

I WAS ABOUT 22 WHEN I started my internship. I got the job with a simple act: I called the main switchboard and asked to be connected with someone with whom I could discuss an internship. I told the man to whom I was transferred that I wanted to be an intern. "What's that?" he asked.

"I work for you and you don't pay me," I explained.

"Come on over," he said.

My gender didn't deter the gentleman with whom I initially spoke and it certainly didn't deter Jeff Birren, the man to whom he directed me, from saying yes to my request. I do not believe it an exaggeration to say that over his approximately 40-year career with the Raiders, Jeff provided more opportunities and encouragement to women (through his internship program and by his mentoring) than did probably every other employee of the league office and all the teams combined.

A few years after I completed my internship, the organization entered an agreement to relocate to Irwindale. As many in the organization were focused on that transaction, a decision was made to hire a new lawyer to work on other business matters (local broadcast agreements, sponsorship deals, licensing issues, and more). Jeff suggested to Al that the organization hire me. Al looked up and said, "Is that the girl?"

"Yes," Jeff said, undoubtedly thinking that not many males are named Amy.

"Okay," Al replied.

That was it. He had no further questions.

He didn't care that I was "the girl." He was simply seeking clarification as to whom Jeff was referring.

IT'S NOT OFTEN SOMEONE JOINS an organization as an intern while in their early 20s, rejoins that same organization as a full-time employee in their mid-twenties, and stays with that same organization until they are over 50 years old.

I grew up while working for the Raiders and for Al.

One of the byproducts of growing up and remaining with one organization for almost three decades is that one grows up, matures and learns on the job and makes a whole heck of a lot of mistakes while so doing. Growing up and learning at the start of one's career doesn't make me different from most other people. What distinguishes my experience from that of many is that I spent almost three decades with one organization so my learning process and the mistakes I made as I grew and as I learned were part of my body of work and followed me throughout my career. I didn't leave my mistakes behind and move on and start fresh with another business.

I imagine many people in business look back at the mistakes they made early in their careers and cringe. I know I do. But not many people are at the same place for over a quarter of a century (almost three decades, if I include my internship). My cringeworthy moments, my mistakes, my missteps were all with one organization.

I offended some people, I bothered some people, I annoyed some people, and I didn't understand until much later how poorly I had handled some situations. I don't have regrets about the substance of the decisions I made and the changes I implemented, but I realized years later that I could have communicated those decisions and implemented those changes more diplomatically. They still – and I still – would have been tremendously unpopular and people would have resisted them no matter what, but I could have trampled fewer feelings.

One of the first significant things I did was to institute a system of internal controls and checks and balances. When I joined the organization, I was stunned at the lack of both. Oh, there was one big check and balance when it came to football operations – his name was Al. But as to business operations, Al wasn't interested in those things, so none existed. Absolutely none. And it was apparent to me that employees, the overwhelming majority of whom had been with the organization for a long time – recognized the lack of internal controls and checks and balances and that some of those employees took advantage of that.

Some employees negotiated agreements that included benefits for themselves. Were those agreements good for the organization? Perhaps, at least in part. Could they have been better for the organization if they did not include provisions benefitting individual employees? I thought so. Should an agreement that contains benefits for the employee who negotiated and signed it be disclosed to and approved by someone else in the organization? Absolutely. Should all agreements (whether or not they contained provisions benefitting employees) be reviewed by counsel? Yes. Some employees directed business to friends and family. Did the business they directed to friends and family need to be performed? In large part, yes. Did those friends and family provide goods or services on commercially appropriate terms? Maybe. Did they do good work? Not always. Should personal connections be disclosed to and approved by someone else in the organization before directing work to friends and family? Absolutely. So although I wasn't directed (or even asked) to address these matters, I did.

There's a certain irony about the fact that I was only able to implement these changes, and to add internal controls and checks and balances, because none existed.

I know that Al had been made aware of what I was doing and he did nothing to deter me.

MY ACTIONS INFURIATED SOME EMPLOYEES. One day, as I was walking through the lobby of our facility, an employee who had been with the organization for a long time, and who patently enjoyed the benefits of working in an environment devoid of controls, shouted at me from across the lobby: "Why don't you just get the fuck out of here, we were fine before you got here and started making changes, and we'll be fine once you're gone – and you'll be gone soon."

Well this was true if by "fine" he meant that employees could act with unfettered autonomy and utilize the assets of the business for their own personal gain without restraint or review.

The need for internal controls, checks and balances, and other changes to the organization's business practices was obvious to me. Instituting such controls and checks and balances and making other systemic changes to the manner in which business was conducted was a satisfying accomplishment.

I was both astonished and disappointed to learn how many people around the league refused to implement such changes in their organizations. They were unwilling to do so, they told me, because they did not want to anger or alienate anyone, which is what I had done. How does that help one's employer? Obviously, it doesn't; it helps only that employee.

As noted earlier, I wouldn't alter the business decisions I made or the changes I implemented, but I could have gone about all of this in a less abrasive manner. I didn't give any thought to the manner in which I communicated these decisions or implemented these changes and I should have. I was the proverbial bull in the china shop. It took me some years to realize that I could have done what I believed to be warranted and necessary more diplomatically.

Efforts at diplomacy would not have helped with all employees, but may well have helped with some. Some employees who were with the organization before I joined were still with it when I left and still resented the changes I made decades earlier. I know this because they were never hesitant to express those views, to me, to Al, and to others.

Quite a few years after I had joined the organization, I learned that one of the most senior employees – a man who had been with the organization for decades before I joined it – referred to me as Cruella De Vil. I learned this because when I returned to the office from a meeting, a coworker told me that I needed to find him, as he'd been looking everywhere for me and asking everyone, "Where's Cruella?"

I never thought about whether the comments shouted across the lobby of our offices for everyone to hear would have been different were I a man. I don't think they would have been. In fact, given the reputation of the man shouting at me, were I a young male employee the comments might well have been accompanied by a shove or a punch. Similarly, I never thought about whether the snarky reference to Cruella was directed at me because of my gender. I don't think it was. Sure, Cruella is a reference to a woman – but had I been a man, his reference would have been to Snidely Whiplash or another male character instead of Cruella.

It's not easy to implement unpopular changes. It's not easy to be the person who says no. It's not easy to do any of this when one is young and learning to lead and it's not easy to do this when employees know that you have no authority to affect their employment status or compensation.

MANY YEARS INTO MY CAREER, the organization was discussing a potential transaction with someone who had tremendous contacts within, and who was in regular contact with, the league office. This man fashioned himself quite influential in league circles. During one meeting, he told me that he was going to share with me something that I would consider insulting, but he believed I should know. It was apparent to me that he wanted me to be insulted, but I was not.

This individual explained that he had been in the league office the day before he came to meet with me and that while in a meeting with several very senior league executives, one said, "Amy does a remarkable job of keeping the circus animals in their rings." He explained that another added: "We don't think anyone else could control all those [circus] animals the way she does."

Insulted? Was he kidding? I was ecstatic. I was thrilled and elated that league officials actually understood the enormity of some of the challenges that existed. I had never shared with or discussed any of these challenges with anyone, as I considered it my responsibility to make us look and be our best and to have moaned about or in any way called attention to the challenges wouldn't have been in the best interests of the organization. So, what this person thought and hoped that I would find insulting, I did not. I considered – and still consider – it a compliment of the highest regard.

We may have been a circus – indeed, in many regards we were – but it was a circus I loved and I was proud and privileged to be part of it. I also cared deeply about those "circus animals."

ANOTHER OF THE MOST SATISFYING projects I undertook concerned both fan behavior and the image of our fans.

Over the years, Raiders fans developed a reputation as rough and inhospitable. They were called thugs and criminals. People warned others not to bring their children to games. Visiting fans weren't safe, others added.

I knew that this image and this reputation were terribly unfair to all the terrific fans and to the tremendous fan base as a whole. The really scary-looking woman with the skull contact lenses? A district attorney.

The frightening-looking man with the crossbones painted on his face? An official with the Department of Homeland Security. Raiders fans are lawyers and contractors, teachers and law-enforcement officials, first responders and landscape engineers, architects and truckers, members of the armed services and farmers, doctors and businesspeople, movie producers and salespeople, musicians and investors, moms and dads, grown-ups and kids, students and professionals, retired and employed, and as a whole, tremendous people.

Were there a small percentage of fans who behaved as what I refer to as knuckleheads and who made game day miserable for those they encountered in the parking lots and in the stadium? Absolutely. While the vast majority of fans of every team are good people, every team has a handful of fans who are knuckleheads and who don't behave appropriately. The Raiders are no different in that regard. The reputation that Raiders fans had garnered was unfair.

I understood the extreme importance of doing two things: (a) making it unequivocally clear that knuckleheads were not welcome – or, stated differently, that inappropriate behavior would not be tolerated; and (b) correcting the misperception about the fan base by making it abundantly clear that those knuckleheads were not representative of Raider Nation as a whole.

In fact, this wasn't simply extremely important, it was essential for the health of the franchise and for the good of the league.

This undertaking was one of my top priorities for a considerable period of time. My goal was to ensure a safe, family- and fan-friendly environment while maintaining the extraordinary home field ambience provided by our fans and to correct the misperception of Raiders fans.

My biggest allies in this undertaking? Raider Nation. These tremendous fans welcomed and embraced these undertakings and goals. They too wanted a safe, family- and fan-friendly environment and they too were angry that the actions of a small group were being attributed to the fan base as a whole. They embraced the fan code of conduct we enacted. In fact, they eagerly and graciously accepted my invitation to participate in the fan conduct videos we showed in-stadium before each game. They embraced the in-stadium texting program we enacted, which allowed fans to report inappropriate behavior from their seats. (It always struck me as idiotic that a terrific fan should have to leave his or her seat to report inappropriate behavior, thus missing chunks of a game, while the knucklehead he or she wished to report didn't miss a down.) Raider fans were vocal proponents of the code of conduct, the texting programs, and all of our other efforts.

As all of our work was in progress, the league took notice. I was delighted with the league's recognition and acknowledgment of our work. I was thrilled when I was asked to serve on the league security committee. Of all of the committees on which I served, this was the most meaningful and satisfying, for a number of reasons.

Interestingly, the biggest and a very substantial challenge to these efforts was presented by individuals very closely related to or associated with ownership. These individuals dismissed the necessity of these initiatives and undermined these efforts in every way imaginable. It infuriated me that the individuals who thwarted these efforts never did what several of my coworkers did at my request: walk in and around and throughout the parking lots and the stadium both before and during each game, spend time in the end zone and the third deck, use the bathrooms the fans use (not the ones in the suites or in the club areas, but all the others throughout the stadium), use a port-a-potty in the parking lot, stand in a concession line. The individuals who dismissed the need for these efforts I believed so important and who undermined them watched from fully catered suites with private restrooms, and they ignored and broke a lot of rules imposed on fans. I did those things every game.

It is not good business for club employees to enter the parking lot via a streamlined, dedicated parking pass lane, park in a protected, secured area, enter the stadium without waiting in security lines and going through security screenings, use only suite and club and employee restrooms, and enjoy the day without ever waiting in a concession line. When invited by the league to speak to a large group of club and league employees who were in San Francisco for a meeting, I shared these thoughts. Club employees (and thus clubs) cannot understand the fan experience if they do not partake in it. To state the obvious, not all fans have parking passes, secured parking, private entrances, private restrooms, and food delivered to them at no cost.

With the help of those employees who understood the importance of and who worked hard on these initiatives and with the tremendous support and invaluable assistance of Raider Nation, who led by example and corrected those whose behavior was unacceptable, we got this done. We succeeded in both regards: families came back in droves (and enjoyed the kids' areas we created), the number of visible visiting-team fans increased, and misperceptions about the fan base were gradually corrected.

I defended Raiders fans my entire career and I shall always passionately do so.

I AM DIRECT AND I communicate in a direct manner. I have been told that I am "direct to a fault." I don't believe that there is such a thing as direct to a fault and I always prefer when people are direct.

That said, there are times I could communicate more diplomatically. But communicating diplomatically and communicating directly are not mutually exclusive and as I grew and I matured, I learned to do both.

On one occasion during my first year with the organization, a fellow employee asked me to come to his office. He was meeting with the representative of a company with whom he was discussing a potential sponsorship deal. They had reached an impasse and they requested my input. I listened to them explain the issues they were unable to resolve and I made suggestions as to how resolve them. I remained with them as they continued their discussion, and it didn't seem to me that they were getting anywhere. The issues they were discussing did not strike me as difficult or complicated, so I said, "Look, this isn't rocket science."

The employee who asked for my advice later told me that I had deeply offended him and the representative of the other company, as they did think that the issues they were discussing were difficult and that I minimized the complexity of the situation.

Notwithstanding that I didn't think it was rocket science, he was right. I could and should have shared my views without being so dismissive and scornful. I could and should have been more diplomatic.

SOME PEOPLE HAVE TOLD ME that my assessment that I would have been better served by being more diplomatic or delicate when instituting these or other changes is gender specific. I don't agree.

I worked with men who assessed themselves and decided that they would be better served to be more diplomatic or delicate. There were times I counseled men to be more diplomatic or delicate. Yes, there were instances in which men counseled me to be more diplomatic or delicate, but I didn't believe their advice to me was any more gender specific than was mine to them.

If men with whom I worked and I made the same observations, whether with respect to ourselves or each other, and if we offered one another the same counsel, then by definition it wasn't gender specific. I believe that we offered one another this advice for the same reason: we wanted one another to be our best and most effective.

I have often heard people state that when a business woman is tough, she is called a bitch, whereas when a business man is tough, he isn't derided in a similar way.

I am troubled by this generalization. I believe it to be a lazy convenience, as many generalizations are.

I have heard people refer to a businessman who is tough as a "dick."

I think it is possible for a woman to be tough without being a bitch, and it is possible for a woman to be a bitch whether she is being tough or not. Similarly, I think it is possible for a man to be tough without being a dick and it is possible for a man to be a dick, whether he is being tough or not. Being tough and being a bitch or a dick are not necessarily correlated, nor are they mutually exclusive.

I am tough and I know that I am reputed to be tough. I don't think that reputation is gender based.

I have done business with both men and women I consider tough and for whom I have tremendous respect.

Some women I respect have shared with me that they have been advised to be nicer and more congenial and that they believe this advice to be gender specific and in contrast with the experience of their male colleagues, none of whom have received such advice. I am not questioning that this was their experience. I do, however, know of men who have received such advice. In fact, I have offered such advice to men.

There were times that I would have been well-advised to be more congenial – not because I was a woman, but because my approach was ineffective. Both men and women can be fairly criticized and well advised to take a more congenial approach at times. I often suggested as much to Al.

Another trait presupposed to be unique to women is the need to be liked or, stated conversely, an aversion to being disliked. Is this unique to women? It is hard for me to believe that all women have trouble with this just as it is hard for me to believe that no men do. I do know that I had to learn to accept not being liked as I progressed within the organization. I was not liked – indeed, I was disliked – by some coworkers and I had to learn to live with that. I was not liked – indeed, I was disliked – by some in the league office and I had to learn to live with that. I was not liked – indeed, I was disliked – by some in with the municipalities with which we had disagreements and I had to learn to live with that. Learning to accept that I would not be liked by everyone was a challenge for me. Early in my career, I would have been bothered by that reference to Cruella. Later in my career, I was most definitely not. But was my early-career aversion to being disliked because I am a woman? I don't believe that was the case. I know men who struggle with not being liked; indeed, I worked with some.

I learned that if I behaved in a manner I believed appropriate and if I did what I thought was right, it was far easier to accept that not everyone liked me than if I did not.

I have been told by women I respect that they strongly disagree with all of these observations. Fair enough; we may have to agree to disagree. As noted, I am not questioning their experiences; I am speaking to mine.

Because my mother and I never discussed the issue of being a woman in business (whether in a male-dominated field or otherwise), I didn't understand or appreciate until well after I began working for the Raiders that my mother's message – and the power thereof – was in what she did not say, rather than in what she said. That is why, when she shared her admiration and appreciation for Al, I immediately stopped what I was doing and listened.

5

"I UNDERSTAND"

I AM OFTEN ASKED WHAT ADVICE I WOULD OFFER YOUNG WOMEN who aspire to, or who have embarked upon, careers in business (particularly in male-dominated fields). My advice to young women is no different than it is to young men: work hard; work really, really, really hard, work as hard as you can, and when you don't believe you can work any harder, work harder.

Working hard matters. A popular phrase for some years has been "work smart." I don't like that expression – I never have. Of course we should work smart but we shouldn't work smart instead of working hard; we should do both. They're not mutually exclusive and they are both important.

So many times, employees would announce that they were able to leave early for the day because they'd "worked smart."

"Really?" I'd respond. "Think how good you could be if you worked smart *and* you worked hard."

And by the way, when something unexpected happens, when an emergency arises and all hell breaks loose, and you're not at the office because you "worked smart" and left, then what sort of teammate are you?

I was once asked by a successful, prominent woman who was the president of a company that was a critical business partner to the Raiders to participate in a fireside chat she was hosting for employees of her company. During the question-and-answer period following our discussion, I was asked what advice I would give a young woman just starting out in business. I explained that my advice to young women is the same as my advice to young men: work hard.

The woman who asked me to join her in this chat gently placed her hand on my arm. "You mean work smart, right?" she said.

Well no, that's not what I meant. But I paused, fully cognizant of the importance to our organization of the relationship between our respective businesses, wondering if I should temper my response. After a beat or two, I responded honestly: "No, I mean work hard." I went on to note that we should aspire to work smart, too, and that working smart and working hard are not mutually exclusive.

So when asked for advice by young women, I share those gender-neutral thoughts about the importance of hard work. And then, I add this advice: stop thinking about the fact that you are a woman.

If a woman doesn't want others to think about her gender, then it makes no sense whatsoever for a woman to think about her gender. If a woman wants to be considered and treated without regard to gender, then she should comport herself without regard to gender. If a woman wants her gender to be irrelevant, then she shouldn't consider it relevant or really, consider it at all. Gender blind means gender blind.

I am frequently asked if I believe I was tested because I am a woman. I don't know, maybe I was. People are tested at different times, for different reasons. What's the best response when one is tested? Pass the test.

I never thought of myself as a woman in business. I never walked into any setting – not a league owners meeting, not a business meeting, not a football operations meeting – thinking about my gender. I didn't think it fair or reasonable or intelligent for me to consider gender if I didn't want others to consider gender. That just never made sense to me. It still doesn't. If others chose to waste their time and energy considering my gender, fine, let them. I certainly was not going to waste mine.

I also don't believe that women should presuppose that they will meet with gender resistance in any or every given situation. Such an assumption can in and of itself be detrimental.

A number of women I respect have shared with me that they do anticipate that they will be treated disparately because they are women.

I understand that in some instances, those women have previously encountered disparate treatment because of their gender and they therefore anticipate that it will be the norm. I'm not suggesting that gender-based resistance (whether discriminatory hiring policies, pay gaps, or otherwise) does not exist. It does, and it's wrong. I am also not suggesting that anyone who is on the receiving end of inappropriate or discriminatory treatment is at fault. Such treatment is unacceptable. I am simply suggesting that I don't believe it's necessarily fair or constructive or productive to presuppose or to assume that gender bias will exist in all environments and in all circumstances before learning that it does. If it does, one can and should then respond as one believes appropriate.

It may be that my views on these topics are generational. I have discussed this subject with many accomplished women who are roughly my age, certainly of my generation, and they have expressed that they too have ignored gender throughout their successful careers and that they too believe that it is counterintuitive to consider one's gender while hoping that others do not. We have considered together that we are a shrinking minority in this respect.

I like my approach to business: that hard work matters, that doing your job matters, that working harder than anyone else matters, that working harder than you ever thought you could matters, and that comporting yourself without regard to gender matters. I don't care that I am a woman. I don't want anyone with whom I work or with whom I interact in business to care that I'm a woman. I don't think about the fact that I am a woman. I don't want anyone with whom I work or interact in business to think about the fact that I'm a woman. I want my gender to be irrelevant. I think that makes all kinds of sense. That approach may not work for everyone, but it worked for me.

Again, I have been told by women I respect that they strongly disagree with these observations. And again, we may have to agree to disagree. As noted, though, I am not questioning their experiences; I am speaking to mine.

I do recognize and appreciate that I had a privilege that many women do not: I worked for a man who afforded me an opportunity notwithstanding my gender. I did my best to make the most of that opportunity. I did so in the manner I believed best.

And that is why Al's words were so significant to me and why I cherish them: *Oh Amy – I swear at Amy – but I don't consider her a woman.*

THIS IS NOT TO SAY that gender-related issues never arose.

Early in my career, when traveling with the team to road games, I was frequently stopped by stadium security when attempting to access certain areas of the stadium.

When our team busses arrived at an away stadium, a hundred or more people – players, coaches, trainers, doctors, equipment and video staff, football staff, business operations staff, and more – poured out and walked toward the tunnel that led to the locker rooms, elevators, stadium innards, and field. I was one of those people.

While everyone else with our traveling party entered the stadium without breaking stride, I was stopped. Sometimes the order to stop was communicated verbally, sometimes I was given the halt gesture, and sometimes someone stepped in front of me, barring my entry. I was always eventually admitted, but only after a strong, hard look at my credential, the same credential worn by my colleagues.

This became a running joke among a group of us. A few of my coworkers stood with me as my credential was scrutinized and we laughed at both the predictability and absurdity of the situation. When officials of the club we were visiting saw what was happening, they rushed to help.

I was also again frequently stopped once we had entered the stadium and were headed toward the field. Again, a few of my coworkers waited with me and again, we shared a laugh. I vividly recall that one instance when security was giving me a particularly hard time, when Gordon Batty, the tremendously respected, legendary trainer of the Green Bay Packers, ran over and intervened. Red, which is what everyone called Gordon, was really angry when he saw that I had been stopped and although he was rushing toward his team bench, he made time to assist me. He didn't have to, but he did and I have long appreciated that.

Why did I laugh instead of shout? I laughed at the predictability and absurdity of this and I laughed at the people who were too dumb to know that the world had changed. I know that I prefer to be yelled at than to be laughed at or ignored. I also knew that I would be granted access.

This stopped happening after my early travels with the team. People learned.

WHILE WRITING THIS BOOK, I spent a wonderful evening with two sensational high school students, both looking to attend college. As I interacted with these young women, I marveled at their poise, composure, intelligence, grace, wisdom, and focus. Had I not known that these young women were in high school, I would have believed them to be well into college or beyond. I certainly didn't possess these characteristics when I was in high school.

I shared with these young women that I was working on a book in which I would share thoughts and stories about my years with the Raiders, and I asked them what they thought I should include in such a book. With no hesitation they began peppering me with a list of topics and questions that were intelligent, insightful, and intriguing.

What was it like to be a woman working for the Raiders? What was it like being a woman in the NFL? What was it like being the first woman to do what I did? Did I think people treated me differently because I was a woman? Did I ever sense that anyone didn't want me doing my job because I was a woman? Did I try to prove anything because I was a woman? Did I try to act a certain way because I was a woman? Did I act differently because I knew I was the first woman in my position? Was it hard to be the first female CEO in the NFL?

Also seated with us were the mothers of these young women. One woman is a highly regarded Superior Court judge and the other an accomplished businesswoman.

Before answering the questions – or really, as part of my answer – I turned to their mothers and asked some questions: Have you ever thought about the fact that you are a woman when you take the bench? When you put on that black robe, do you consider yourself a female judge or simply a judge? Have you ever thought about the fact that you are a woman when instructing a jury, sentencing someone, or holding someone in contempt? Do you think about the fact that you are a woman when running a business? When meeting with bankers? Have either of you ever thought about the fact that you are women when doing any aspect of your respective jobs? The answer to each question was no. These women and I are approximately the same age.

I turned to the two students and said: "I did my job, your moms do theirs. I worked as hard as I could, as do your moms. That's it. I didn't waste my time or energy worrying about my gender or the concerns of others, and neither do your moms. If others are concerned, let them waste their time and energy with such concerns." The mothers nodded in agreement and smiled. I found it fascinating that these young women were so interested in this topic. I also found it fascinating to watch them absorb everything we shared with them.

THERE WAS ONE TIME THAT I chose to share a gender-related story with Al. I hadn't thought about this moment for ages, until sitting down to write this book.

I had read a powerful story involving our military. I can't remember where I found this story and I don't know whether it was precisely written or whether it was embellished. I do know that I found it in what I believed to be a credible publication.

As I was reading the story, I had an immediate and overwhelming urge to share it with Al and the moment I finished, I rushed across the hall to his office to do so. It was late in the evening – well after the time we normally finished our post-practice discussions – and I sat down to wait for him as he finished speaking with another staff member. As that person was walking out, I told Al that I wanted to read something to him. He started to stop me, but I began reading and either the tone of my voice or the first sentence of what I was reading, or both, struck him, and he sat back in his chair and allowed me to read the entire, fairly long story aloud. I know I won't recount this military incident as beautifully as did the writer, but the story was basically this:

Fighting had been underway for hours, our forces were taking heavy fire, and we were suffering tremendous casualties. One of our planes was shot down very close to the enemy. A radio call from the pilot let us know where he was and how much time he thought he would have before the enemy reached him. A call went out asking whether there was anybody close to him with the fuel to get to him and what sort of ordnance they had. A number of pilots, all of whom wanted to help, responded immediately and reported that they were too far away, didn't have enough fuel, or didn't have any ordnance. Then, an army helicopter pilot came on the radio and said: here's my location, I have this much fuel, I can be to him in this many minutes, I have no ordnance. I'm going to get him.

I will never forget her voice. I would follow her into combat anywhere, anytime.

As I finished reading the story, my voice was quivering substantially and I had goosebumps and a lump in my throat, as I do now. I looked at Al and the expression on his face was warm and understanding. He said, "I understand." That was it: *I understand.*

To this day, I don't know why it was so important to me to share that story with Al, but it was. I just know that the story touched me deeply and I wanted to share it with him. Perhaps it was my way of letting him know that, although we had never spoken about it, I appreciated that he provided me with the opportunity he did. That was a moment I will never forget.

6

"SHE'S NOT A GIRL, SHE'S A RAIDER"

IT DIDN'T OCCUR TO ME THAT ANYONE OUTSIDE OF THE RAIDERS, the league office, or other clubs knew of my role with the organization.

Early in my career, when we were in Philadelphia to play the Eagles, I learned in a surprising and wonderful way that some others did.

As I sat with other Raiders staff in the visiting-team section of the press box just before kickoff, I felt a brush against my ear and I heard a voice whisper: "I'm so excited that you're doing what you're doing, that you're in the league. It's perfect that you are with the Raiders. If I can ever help you, let me know." The person who whispered that then immediately began walking away. As she did, I turned my head and saw that it was Lesley Visser. All I could think was: *Holy crap, how in the hell does Lesley Visser know who I am?*

I remember her words all these years later and I can hear her voice as I write this.

Lesley is the woman who first did so many of the things that women in sports media now do. There have been few in sports journalism – male or female – who have accomplished or achieved what she has. Lesley is the first woman in the Pro Football Hall of Fame and she is the only woman who has presented the Lombardi Trophy to the Super Bowl winner.

When Lesley shared those sensational words with me, I was stunned and overwhelmed.

Lesley was tremendous to me throughout my career; she supported me and encouraged me in every conceivable manner. She does that to this day. No matter how many times I have tried to do so, I don't believe that

I have adequately conveyed to Lesley the impact on me of her words and her support and encouragement.

Many years after I met Lesley, she shared with me that the first time she was credentialed to enter an NFL locker room, her credential included the standard disclosure that women were not allowed in the locker room. That prohibition on her credential was inconsequential to Lesley; she wasted no time considering it; she was not deterred; she was undaunted. Lesley had been given an assignment and she did it magnificently, as she always does.

Al had tremendous admiration for Lesley and he spoke to me often about her throughout my career. Not many people impressed Al; Lesley did.

Another woman I met early in my career is Andrea Kremer. I met Andrea at one of the first league meetings I attended. It may have been the very first. There was always a rush for the bathroom at breaks in the meeting; everyone made an immediate beeline for them. When I walked into the women's room, there was one other person there. It was Andrea – an outstanding, accomplished, award-winning, formidable journalist. Andrea was an intimidating presence (she scared the crap out of me, that's for sure) and there she was in the women's room.

The restroom was quiet – it was just the two of us. In an effort to break what I believed to be an awkward silence (it was awkward for me, that's for sure), I said the only thing that came to mind: "Well, there's no line in the women's room at these meetings, that's a nice thing." We both laughed at how, for once, the women's restroom was practically empty while there was a long line for the men's room. Even when I resigned, decades later, when there were other women in the league, there still weren't enough to cause a line. As for my restroom meeting with Andrea, it was my great fortune. Andrea offered me support and encouragement throughout my career as she does to this day. Andrea sets a tremendous example and is a fierce advocate for women in media, sports, and otherwise.

Also early in my career, Georgia Frontiere, Carroll Rosenbloom's widow and the owner of the Rams, approached me at a league social function. When she located me, Georgia explained that she had made a point of finding me so that she could tell me that she was excited to see a woman who was not related to ownership with a team and to offer her support. I was stunned that Georgia knew who I was and that she went to such an effort to locate me and to offer her encouragement. I was impressed by her graciousness and generosity.

When I reflect upon Georgia's graciousness and when I consider the support and encouragement Lesley and Andrea provided me over the course of my career (and that they still provide), I think about the maxim that women have a responsibility to support other women.

The fact that these women supported and encouraged me is not lost on me when I share my view that I don't believe that women should support and encourage other women simply because they are women. To do so is not consistent with a gender-blind approach.

Over the course of my career, I received support and encouragement from both women and men and I have offered my support and encouragement to both women and men.

I support and encourage women when support and encouragement are warranted. I support and encourage men when support and encouragement are warranted. I don't think it's fair for me to consider gender when interacting with others if I want others to interact with me without regard to mine.

If we want men to treat us without regard to gender, then it strikes me as logical and right that we treat men without regard to gender. After all, gender blind is gender blind.

I'M NOT SUGGESTING THAT I didn't meet with any resistance during my career. Some of that resistance came from within the organization and some from outside of it.

Some very prominent men – some of whom are in the Hall of Fame, some of whom were or still are associated with the Raiders, and some of whom never were – attempted for years to get Al to fire me. I know this because Al told me. He would giggle as he told me of the former coach, the former personnel executive, and a number of others who periodically urged him to get rid of me.

Yes, Al giggled.

Was some of that resistance gender based? I don't know. I never spent any time considering whether or not it was. Over the years, a number of men and women I respect have shared with me that they did and they do believe that such resistance was gender based. Somewhat recently, a few tremendously accomplished, successful women shared with me experiences they had with one of these men in particular, experiences which astonished me and which most certainly suggest gender bias. If this man communicated to these women that they weren't welcome in meetings in which their male counterparts were welcome and that they were not qualified to do their jobs because of their gender, then it's certainly plausible to think that he may have held the same views about me. So some of this resistance may have been gender-based. But if gender was the cause of such resistance, would I have changed my approach or conducted myself any differently? I am certain that the answer to that question is no.

I have been told that I should have expressed an objection or protested any time I perceived a gender-based slight. The best protest is to succeed. My time and energy was best spent focusing on doing my job as best I could.

Many people are surprised when I tell them that I never experienced what I believed to be any gender-based resistance from players, whether Raiders or those on other teams. Although others find this surprising, I do not. Players evaluate their teammates and others on performance. Are you blocking your man? Are you covering your receiver? Are you doing your job? Of course I recognize that Raiders players were aware of my working relationship with Al and the confidence he had in me, but that was not the case with all players throughout the league and yet they too accepted me without regard to gender. When I left, I was touched by how many former and current players contacted me – far more than I would ever have imagined.

One incident in which my gender was alluded to stands out, perhaps because I was surprised by the hypocrisy of it. Sometime not too long after DeMaurice Smith was first elected head of the players' association, he and a group of union employees visited our facility to meet with our players. DeMaurice wished to speak with Al, but Al was unavailable and he asked me to greet DeMaurice in his stead.

As I approached DeMaurice, one of the men in his group stepped between us, in what was an obvious effort to block me from DeMaurice and to keep me from speaking to him. As he inserted himself between us, this union employee asked: "Whose secretary are you?" Now this was 2009 or 2010. But whether it was 2009 or 2010, it was not 1940 or 1950. *Whose secretary are you?*

I just stared at him.

As I stood there stunned, considering how to proceed, Nolan Harrison (also a union employee and a former Raider) spotted me from across the room where he was speaking with a player, rushed over, and wrapped me in a giant hug.

I don't know whether Nolan had noticed the interaction just described or whether he rushed over simply because he saw me and wanted to say hello.

Nolan introduced me to the group of union employees, including the man who blocked me from introducing myself to DeMaurice. That man stepped aside – a smidge – but he didn't say anything, not a word. So let's get this straight: the union – the very organization that advocates that owners and management should treat its members respectfully and professionally (which they should) – had on its staff at least one person who concluded that because I am a woman, I must have been someone's secretary? What did that tell me about the union leadership at that time? It told me that while advocating for respect for some, they weren't affording that to all.

As a quick aside, my history with Nolan involved the police and a gun aimed at me. I know that Nolan will not object to me sharing this story, as the only law he *may* have broken was that he *may* have been driving a bit over the speed limit, but no speeding ticket was issued. It was September 1994. We had played our season opener on a Monday night, in San Francisco. During the game, one of our players, Napoleon McCallum, suffered a terrible injury. I was told at the time it was life-threatening. I remember Napoleon laying on the field and Ken Norton Jr., who had tackled Napoleon, lying absolutely still under him for what seemed to be an eternity. Our medical staff had advised Ken that it was imperative that he stay absolutely still while they worked to stabilize Napoleon's leg so that he could be transported to the hospital. Ken did not move and he did his best to keep Napoleon's leg from moving. I've had a soft spot for Ken Norton Jr. since that day.

We lost the game – badly. Jerry Rice set all sorts of records. It was a long night. We arrived back at the Los Angeles International Airport in the early-morning hours on Tuesday and then went to our facility to get our cars. As I was driving home, I saw police lights in my rearview mirror and immediately experienced that stomach-in-your-mouth feeling that you get when you think you are getting a ticket. I noticed, though, that there was a car between mine and the police car and I quickly realized that it was one of our players. It was Nolan.

I immediately pulled to the side of the road just in front of Nolan, jumped from my car, and started running towards the policeman as he was approaching Nolan's car. The officer immediately drew his gun, pointed it directly at me, and commanded me to stop where I was and to display my hands, which I did.

It certainly wasn't unreasonable for a policeman to be concerned that someone running towards him in that situation might be armed. Even a small woman can have a gun.

I stopped dead in my tracks and I began speaking very quickly – even more quickly than I normally speak. I was blabbering that we had just played – and lost – a very emotional football game, that one of our teammates suffered a gruesome injury and was hospitalized in San Francisco. I just kept talking and talking. At one point, I looked at Nolan through the windshield of his car and saw him laughing, but trying not to let me see that he was. The officer holstered his gun. I thought that was a good sign so I approached him – more slowly this time – and I talked some more. Nolan just watched and smiled. Nolan didn't get a ticket. I didn't get shot.

So it was fitting that Nolan was present when the union representative was barring my path to DeMaurice. I'll note though, that Nolan did not have to face a gun, as I did when I assisted him.

ONE SILLY INSTANCE IN WHICH my gender was an issue involved a game of indoor football. Not too long after we relocated to Oakland and moved into our new facility, a group of us were relaxing in the hallway. Someone had a Nerf football and we started tossing it around. We then decided to have an impromptu, indoor football game. I grabbed the ball and said to Jim Otto: "Hey Jim, why don't you be the center?"

I'm quite a scout. I chose the Hall of Fame center, whom the *Sporting News* named as one of the top 100 best players of all time, to be the center in our indoor Nerf football game. Jim centered the ball and as I walked up to take the snap from under center, he started screaming "shotgun, shotgun, shotgun" in a somewhat high-pitched, shrill tone. Well, that was funny because as those who follow the Raiders know, the Raiders eschewed the shotgun formation, preferring instead to have the quarterback up under center. So, when Jim shouted *shotgun*, we all knew why he did – he didn't want me up under center. We all laughed and agreed that this most certainly must have been the first time in the hallowed halls of the Raiders – literally, the halls – that someone had called for a shotgun formation.

Jim played his first season for the Raiders in 1960, the year before I was born. There were no women involved in football during those years. Over the course of his life and his career, times had changed. Like Willie Brown, Jim and many others were experiencing a paradigm shift. Yet never once during my career did Willie or Jim or other Hall of Fame Raiders from a different era – Ted Hendricks, Gene Upshaw, George Blanda, Art Shell, or Fred Biletnikoff – seem bothered by my gender. We didn't always agree about business matters. We had different views on a number of issues. Yet these men conducted themselves as if my gender was irrelevant. Jim just didn't want me up under center. He wanted me in shotgun.

Again, I recognize that these men, like current players, were aware of my working relationship with Al and the confidence he had in me, but these were older, Hall of Fame players who did not have to concern themselves with "the boss's" views.

NOT EVERY REFERENCE TO MY gender was as inconsequential. I found it both surprising and interesting that when I joined the organization, the strongest resistance I encountered was from the media covering the Raiders at that time. I was also surprised by the intensity of that resistance.

I was about 11 years old at the time of the Watergate break-in and I grew up with a tremendous respect for journalists and an appreciation for the importance of the fourth estate. I considered journalism a noble profession, and for a period of time considered becoming a journalist. I think that it is because I held journalists in such high regard that I was as surprised as I was by this resistance.

Over the years, when I have shared with female journalists and women in the media that I was surprised by the level of resistance from their male counterparts, they have looked at me as if I were nuts, and they have laughed. These women experienced this resistance on a regular basis. It was their reality. For some women, this still is their reality. I have a better understanding of this now than I did during my years with the Raiders and certainly, a much better understanding than I did when I began my career.

One day very early in my career, I walked outside to the practice field to share some news with Al. It was toward the end of practice and as I waited on the sideline for an opening to speak with him, I stood near Gene Upshaw, who was watching practice that day. Gene was one of the best offensive linemen in the history of football, a Hall of Fame player, and a Raider – a true Raider. He passed away in 2008.

A group of writers stood near us and one walked closer and asked Gene in a very loud voice, clearly intended to carry, "What's it like having a girl working for the team?"

Gene towered over most people at 6'5" and 255 pounds. Standing next to Gene was like standing next to a pillar of granite. He looked as if he were chiseled from stone. His glare could wither people.

Gene looked down at this writer and in an even louder, booming voice said: "She's not a girl, she's a Raider."

7

GET THE
SANDWICHES

I'VE BEEN ASKED MANY TIMES TO NAME MY FAVORITE PLAYER. I have never done so, I will not do so, and even if I were to do so, my favorite player is someone I don't think anyone would know.

Very early in my career the then-most senior person in our player personnel department rushed into my office. He was quite flustered. He shoved a player contract towards me and pointed to a portion of it. "I need you to supersede this," he said.

Player contracts are collectively bargained and mostly standardized. I didn't work on player contracts and the man standing before me waving the contract knew that. "Supersede what?" I asked.

Again, he thrust the contract towards me. "We need to supersede this," he said, "we need a supersede clause."

"We need to supersede what?" I again asked.

"We need to supersede all of this," he responded, shaking the page at me and pointing to a number of paragraphs.

He explained a bit more, so thinking that I understood what he wanted, I drafted an addendum, superseding the entirety of what I believed he wished me to supersede. I had myself a little supersede party.

Late that night – just before midnight – my home phone rang. It was Al. I believe that was the first time he ever called me at home. It know it was the first time he ever called me at midnight.

"Amy, this is Al Davis," he began, as if I weren't able to recognize his voice. He went on to ask why "the fuck" I had converted a standard player contract into a guaranteed, no-cut, no-trade contract.

We had brought the player in question in to fill an open spot at the bottom of the roster. As is said in football, he was "just a guy." After we worked him out, we signed him to a contract. I turned that contract into a guaranteed, no-cut, no-trade contract. Oops.

I replied that I understood both the mistake that I made and the magnitude of it. Al was not impressed – in fact, he wasn't interested. I did not explain why I did what I did and I did not belabor our discussion with an explanation of the questions I had asked when I was instructed to draft the supersede provision earlier that day. I asked Al what, if anything, I could do to fix my mistake. I was terrified that the answer would be "nothing."

But there was a solution. The employee who had asked me to draft the supersede provision and who told Al of my error had reached the player at his hotel and requested that he rip up that contract and sign a new one. The player was flying out early the next morning, but agreed to come to our offices at 5:00 AM to sign a new contract.

I got to the office at 4:00 AM to await him. I almost went at midnight to just sit there and wait.

This player – this honorable, ethical, wonderful man – may well have saved my job and I may well have gone on to have the career I did because he bailed me out. To others he may have been "just a guy." Well, to me, he wasn't just a guy. He was then, he still is, and he shall always be to me in my personal hall of fame. He's my favorite player. I thanked him profusely. I think I hugged him – it certainly would have been in character for me to do so.

That was my first late-night call with Al. Looking back on it years later, I could not – and I still cannot – believe that he when he spoke to me, he was as controlled and patient as he was. Perhaps this interaction suggested to Al that I would not recoil when he very directly pointed out mistakes, that I would not worry about who was at fault but instead, would work to fix problems as best I could.

Another player who has a very special place in my heart and my marriage is Greg Townsend.

My husband and I were married after I completed my internship but before I joined the organization on a full-time basis. Although I was not employed by the Raiders at the time, I did consider the football schedule when selecting the date and time for our wedding.

We chose a Sunday night in December – back then, there was no Sunday night football and our wedding was to begin well after the team's game in Denver concluded. I didn't count on overtime.

We were at the wedding venue and I was in a room with our matron of honor, bridesmaids, and other family and friends. They were all urging me to get ready – to do my hair, do my makeup, and get dressed. Well, I was watching the game and I refused to get ready until it ended. The game was tied at 14 at the end of regulation. I still refused to do hair and makeup. The game wasn't over – I wanted to watch overtime.

In overtime, Greg recovered a John Elway fumble, and the Raiders kicked a field goal and won the game. Game over – time to get married. At this point, there really wasn't time for a whole lot of attention to hair and makeup – so I ran a brush through my hair; put on mascara, lipstick, and my dress; and walked down the aisle.

For years, a story circulated that I was late for my own wedding so that I could watch a game. That's not true. I was not late for the wedding. I was perfectly on time walking down the aisle. I was, however, a bride without fancy hair and makeup – but I was in an especially happy mood, as the Raiders won the game. I shared this story with Greg, and we had fun over the years referring to it. At one big event at which I introduced Greg, I did so by saying that I was proud and pleased to introduce "a man who had a very special role in making me very happy on my wedding night." The looks on the audience's faces when I then called Greg up to the stage were priceless. I went on to share the story and to explain why both my husband and I appreciated Greg's role in winning that game.

I EARLIER RECOUNTED A STORY in which someone in the league office referenced circus animals when discussing our organization. That analogy was not intended as a compliment, but was in many respects fair. There were, however, times when we were a circus in the best sense of that word: we were a lot of fun and we could be entertaining.

On one instance, I was traveling to a league meeting with two others on Raiders staff, one of whom was the most senior executive in our player personnel department, the other in our finance department. We were on a flight to New York and after finishing a few work projects, I decided to watch a movie: *Free Willy*.

At the end of the movie, when Willy (the whale) leapt over the rock wall separating him from the ocean, I started crying. Well not just crying, sobbing.

The personnel executive who was seated a few rows behind me and on the opposite side of the plane stood up and yelled to our other colleague, "Hey, look at fuckin' Amy, she's crying."

His tone was lighthearted and he sounded both surprised and amused. I remember thinking: *I'm sure everyone sitting anywhere near us wants to listen to his commentary; it's bad enough that they've had to listen to me sobbing.*

I wasn't embarrassed. I remember thinking, though, that we were a pretty entertaining or, to those wishing to work or to sleep, annoying traveling group.

Another in-flight movie moment may have also entertained some passengers. I was traveling with Al to a league meeting and after finishing something we were working on partway into the flight, I decided to watch *The Jungle Book*. I didn't hear Al trying to get my attention, so he asked the man in the row between us for assistance. When that man tapped me on the shoulder, he pointed to Al, and said "I told him you were watching *The Jungle Book*, but he wants to speak to you anyway," I remember thinking: *You didn't really have to tell him it was* The Jungle Book, *did you?* Then, I heard Al say, "Fuck, she's watching the fuckin' *Jungle Book*." He sounded perplexed.

Al was perplexed and concerned on another cross-country flight as four of us traveled home from the league office. The trip had been stressful, particularly for our lead lawyer, Jeff. To unwind, he decided to watch *Home Alone 2* and I joined him. The movie wasn't that great but the two of us giggled uncontrollably, like elementary school kids at a sleepover. So much so that Al told the fourth person in our traveling party to go check on us, explaining to him that "something's wrong with them."

Al was an easy traveler in many regards. When traveling up and down the state of California, for example, he chose to fly a commuter airline – it had no first class – and, in fact, no assigned seats. The airline let Al board first and he always chose to sit in the first row. He brought his own lunch in a brown paper bag (most frequently, a tuna sandwich). One time, Snoop Dogg's father boarded and, upon seeing Al in his seat, extended his hand and introduced himself by his first name. Al immediately extended his hand and very politely said, "Nice to meet you, Mr. Dogg." Seated immediately behind him, I kicked his chair and hissed: "It's not Mr. Dogg. Snoop's last name isn't even Dogg, it's Broadus, this is *not* 'Mr. Dogg.'"

We were an entertaining travel group.

I'VE NOTED SEVERAL TIMES THAT Al giggled. And he did. He also sang. Al loved a certain genre of music – not the genre one would normally associate with football – and not the genre one might associate with Al. Gloria Loring was one of his favorites, as was Ann Margret. Each season, Al wanted to be sure that we extended an invitation to Gloria and Ann to sing the anthem at a game. He loved it when they did. Each season, young employees flocked to my office to plead with me not to extend the invitations to those women. I said: "they're singing."

One of Al's favorite songs was by Frank Sinatra: "My Way." Al sang that refrain often. Sometimes, he'd sing it just because he was relaxed and in the mood to sing. Sometimes, he'd sing it as I sat in his office, wondering how the hell I could get him to focus on the topic at hand, instead of singing. Sometimes, he'd sing it after we had disagreed about something, as I was walking out of his office. He did it in a silly manner – to tease me – to let me know in a warm way that we were going to do something his way.

"Yes, I get it. We'll do it your way," I'd respond. And then, while walking out, I'd mutter (loudly, so that Al would hear), "As usual."

That song was perfect for Al. Al did it his way when on two occasions he refused to allow his team to play in the segregated South. His refusal to participate in those games resulted in them being moved to cities that were not segregated and in which all players could stay in the same hotel. He did it his way when he hired Tom Flores, and then me, and then Art Shell. He did a lot of things his way to which many people objected. He should be remembered for the groundbreaking things he did his way.

Al wasn't someone who just talked about equality. He demonstrated his beliefs with actions, over decades.

Periodically, I'd suggest to Al that we let the public know more about the instances in which he moved those games from segregated cities and that we let the public know more about his decades-long practice of diverse and inclusive hiring. But he refused to discuss – or to allow me to discuss – these things publicly. Each time I suggested we do so, he sternly admonished me. "Hey, lemme get something straight with you, young lady" he'd say. "I didn't do it for publicity."

"I know you didn't do it for publicity," I'd groan. "That's the point." I went on to note that it was precisely because he did these things for all the right reasons, that it was so important. Then I'd plead, "But can't we get just a little bit of positive recognition for you? That would really help," I would moan.

He'd refuse again. No matter how often I suggested this – pleaded with him about this – he refused.

Although his refusal to allow me to garner some positive attention for his lifelong commitment to diversity and inclusiveness frustrated me to no end during my years with the team, I realized that this too was what made Al, Al. He did it; he did not want to talk about it. That's rare.

EARLY IN MY CAREER, THE organization was involved in some routine insurance litigation. It wasn't sexy or interesting and I wasn't particularly involved but on the day Al was to be deposed, as he began walking toward his car to head to that deposition, he said to me: "Let's go, Trask."

It had never occurred to me that he would want me with him, but he did. I grabbed my things and joined the group headed to the deposition, which was to be conducted at a law firm.

The deposition had been underway for several hours when the lawyer deposing Al asked him if he wanted to break for lunch. Al responded no, he had things to do and wanted to work through lunch but if others wanted to eat, someone could bring sandwiches in, and they could eat while they continued the deposition.

The lawyer's response: "Oh, good idea. Amy can get the sandwiches."

Al immediately banged his hand down on the table, his pinky ring clanging loudly. "Did you hear that? Did you hear that?" he said, looking up and down the long conference table, addressing everyone in attendance. "There's one woman in this room and this guy says, 'Amy can get the sandwiches.' Did you hear that? This guy is really something."

This wasn't for show. Al was really angry. At the other end of the table, I sat there with a big smile on my face.

Al then said to my supervisor, the man who had hired me, the organization's chief lawyer who ultimately became its general counsel: "Jeff, get the sandwiches." To this day, Jeff and I love to laugh about this, and we periodically say to one another, "Jeff, get the sandwiches" as a wonderful tribute to Al.

I recognize that I had the privilege of working for a man who was not only unconcerned with my gender, but who spoke up and criticized others when he thought that they were too concerned with it. I realize that not all women have this privilege or this luxury. Did Al's lack of concern with my gender – and his defense of me when he believed it was of concern to others – shape my views on comporting myself without regard to gender? No, it did not shape them. But Al's views did create an environment which made it far easier for me to conduct myself as I wished than would have been the case elsewhere. Of course I understand that.

A HUMOROUS DEPOSITION MOMENT OCCURRED when Al was called upon to testify in a case about a game-day slip-and-fall matter. Again, I wasn't planning to attend but again, on his way to the deposition, he said "Trask, let's go," so I did. When we sat down to begin the deposition, I noticed two very young men in the room and I asked who they were. The lawyer who was to depose Al explained that one was his son, and another was his son's friend. "Are you kidding?" I asked. "Did you sell tickets?" I went on to pitch a bit of a fit, noting that his right to depose Al did not give him the right to use the deposition to entertain family and friends. Al was not as bothered as I was – he was more tolerant of such things, which was interesting – and he told me to calm down. Once the kids were gone, the lawyer began the deposition and one of the first things he asked Al was whether he had ever been seen in the presence of large men in sweat pants. Al looked at Jeff, who was defending him in this deposition, and said, "Does this guy know what I do?"

WHILE ON THE TOPIC OF litigation, I will note that although I attended law school, I did so with the express, stated intent of never practicing law. I wanted a legal education and a law degree for a number of reasons, but not so that I could be a lawyer. I pledged that not only wouldn't I ever see the inside of a courtroom, I wouldn't even know how to find the courthouse.

Upon graduation, I did join a law firm and I practiced transactional law (to wit: not litigation) for a short period of time but I still proclaimed that I would never see the inside of a courtroom or even be able to find the courthouse. That changed, of course, when I joined the Raiders.

The organization was embroiled in litigation well before I joined it and remained involved in litigation for a number of years thereafter. Although I never represented the organization in these matters or otherwise served as a litigator, I did attend some hearings to observe and in some matters, I was called as a witness. So, although I vowed that I would never find or enter that courthouse, I did.

On one occasion, without considering what I was about to do, I actually acted as a trial lawyer. We were in trial with the NFL and it was my turn on the witness stand. The lawyer for the league had been questioning me for a quite awhile, and then said: "I want to ask you a question." *What a stupid thing to say*, I thought. *I'm on the witness stand; the only reason I'm here is so that you can ask me questions; you've been questioning me for some time; you don't need to tell me that you want to ask me a question.* Then, he asked his question, only it was two questions in one. I responded instinctively and said, "Actually, that was two questions, not one." I hadn't intended to pose an objection or to pretend I was a trial lawyer; I said what I did because he was annoying me and he said something I thought was dumb. The judge immediately said, "Objection sustained." *Hey, look at me*, I thought; *I just made my very first (and I hope only) objection and it was sustained.* I am sure I was smiling broadly. I looked into the audience where Al and my husband were sitting and they were both doing all they could to keep from laughing too hard – but they were laughing pretty hard.

I NOTED EARLIER THAT MY first late-night call from Al came when I turned a standard player contract into a guaranteed, no-cut, no-trade contract. Another of what were many middle-of-the-night calls concerned *Beavis and Butt-head*, the MTV cartoon.

One night, after my husband and I had gone to bed and were well on our way to falling asleep, the phone rang. It was after midnight and we looked at one another knowingly – it was Al. My husband recalls my end of the conversation like this:

"No…Beavis. BEE–VIS. No. Beavis. Like beaver, only Beavis. Mmm hmm. Beavis. Yes, Butt-head. BUTT HEAD. Like two words – butt and head – only one – Butt-head. That's right" Then, just for fun and added effect, I then intoned, "heh, heh, heh, heh" just the way Beavis or Butt-head said it.

Well at this point, my husband looked at me like I lost my mind, rolled over, and went to sleep. Fortunately, he can sleep through anything.

We had received in discovery in our litigation with the league a copy of a league memorandum in which a very senior league executive referred to a group of team owners as "Beavis and Butt-head owners." So, I had to explain to Al who Beavis and Butt-head were and that this was not a compliment (which, really, one should have understood from the name Butt-head). That week, I bought a VHS of *Beavis and Butt-head* and gave it Al. I don't think he ever watched it.

NOT ALL MIDNIGHT CALLS WERE as humorous as the one in which I explained Beavis and Butt-head to Al.

Throughout my career, Al began each of what I call his midnight calls by saying "Amy, this is Al," or "Amy, this is Al Davis," as if I wouldn't recognize his voice. I could tell by the tone he used when he did so what the tenor of the call would be.

Sometimes, Al called simply to catch up, discuss business, or have a conversation. I enjoyed these calls; they were relaxed and enjoyable. On those calls, we often talked about football – player personnel, game matchups, play calling, his theories of football. Also on those calls, we discussed world affairs and current events. I recall once discussing with him at length the funeral of Yasser Arafat and what impact his death would have on the world.

Most often, though, when Al called me late at night it was because he was concerned about something, focused on something, working on a matter of importance to the club, angry about something or at someone, or mad at me. Quite often, he was already angry when he called. Other times, he was not angry when he called, but by the time we were done he sure was. We discussed transactions we were working on, deals we were negotiating, financial matters, and other significant business issues, and we often disagreed as to how address these matters. Al motherfucked me a lot during these calls. Sometimes he directed his motherfucking at others, like coaches and league executives. But even in those instances in which his motherfucking was directed at others, he made sure to include me as well.

One night, during a particularly stressful time when Al's middle of the night motherfuckings were more frequent than usual, I recall walking into our kitchen and seeing my husband reading a 10-K. I crinkled my nose and told him that I didn't understand how he could do that, noting that reading regulatory filings is "boring." He responded by waving the document in the air and noting that 10-Ks didn't call him in the middle of the night and motherfuck him. I acknowledged that he had a good point.

JUST AS AL STOOD UP for me when it was suggested that I get the sandwiches, he defended me in other ways.

One notable moment came after an incident that occurred at what the league calls a "small group owners meeting." In this instance, the small group owners' meeting was the night before a two-per-club meeting scheduled for the following day. Small group owners meetings are designed to foster intimate conversations between owners on sensitive issues. I always found the mixture of clubs assigned to each small group owners meetings interesting. Sometimes clubs were grouped by division or geography, but on other occasions the groupings were not divisional or geographic but, rather, intended to be strategic.

Over the course of my career, Al increasingly chose not to attend league meetings and sent me in his place. In instances in which more than one representative per club was permitted, I most often brought a coworker with me. Small group owners meetings were limited to one participant per club. For most clubs, that participant was the owner.

At this particular meeting, an owner leveled some false and troubling accusations and launched an ad hominem attack.

Look, I have no aversion to arguments. Arguments can be productive. Arguments can help solve problems. Sharing views in a forthright, honest, direct manner, in an animated, spirited, or heated fashion, can lead to good results. It's okay to be loud; it's okay to get angry. People should feel welcome to argue. If at the end of an argument an agreement or understanding hasn't been reached, then agree to disagree, understanding that reasonable minds can differ.

As one Raiders coach once told the media when they asked him about an argument on our sideline during a game: "There's no sign on our sideline that says *no yelling.*" I loved that. I think that approach should apply in business environments too.

Reasoned and reasonable arguments intended to problem solve can be valuable. I don't believe, however, that such arguments should ever include ad hominem attacks.

Did I argue during my career? You bet I did. Did I raise my voice and share my views in a loud and heated manner? I sure did. Did I argue more than some would have liked or more than some thought appropriate? I am sure that I did. Looking back, do I think that there were times that a less argumentative approach may have been better? Sure. But I never attacked anyone on a personal level.

The argument at this small group owners meeting wasn't really an argument; it was something different.

This owner's rage was palpable. I remember actually thinking at one point while he was at full throttle that he might pop a blood vessel.

He criticized the organization for not doing all that it could, or even taking reasonable steps, to maximize revenues and for making business decisions without regard to the financial ramifications thereof, all the while accepting – indeed, relying upon – a revenue sharing subsidy from those clubs which did those things and thus maximized their revenues. He was right. I agreed with his assessment in its entirety and I had argued with Al about these very things for decades.

I had tried repeatedly and unsuccessfully to convince Al over the course of many years that it was intellectually dishonest to refuse to engage in business practices designed to increase our revenues – like opening training camp to ticket holders, providing sponsors and other business partners access to him, providing access to coaches and players – all the while accepting and relying upon a subsidy from those clubs that were doing the very things he refused to do. I explained again and again that it was disingenuous to refuse to engage in certain marketing activities because he believed that they were bad for our football team, and yet take money from clubs that engaged in those activities. After all, I'd point out, according to his logic, the organizations engaging in those business practices were doing so to the detriment of their football teams in order to maximize their revenues and although he refused to do the same, he accepted and relied upon a subsidy from them. We fought about this for years. Al never offered what I considered a reasonable response.

Had this shouting owner been willing to listen to me – had he been willing to engage in a dialogue and to exchange thoughts and ideas (whether in raised tones or not) – he would have learned that I agreed with him, that I had articulated those very criticisms to Al, and that I had told Al that other owners were right to be angry.

The whole time that owner was screaming at me, none of the league executives intervened – and they shouldn't have. I don't believe that they would have intervened were I male, so good for them that they didn't. I'm glad no one assisted me. That's how it should have been.

But then, this owner leveled one accusation which was wrong and which infuriated me: he declared that I forced Al to do things, that I controlled Al. Had I not been rendered speechless by his absurd accusation and the fury in his voice when he expressed them – I may well have simply laughed at him. Al was a lot of things – controllable was not one of them.

This owner asserted that I was responsible for all of Al's bad decisions. "You made Al move the team back to Oakland," he yelled at one point. I made Al move the team? Wow. He sure thought I was powerful. In hindsight, I decided that perhaps I should have been flattered that he thought I had such power over a man everyone knew couldn't be controlled.

This owner never asked me anything about the move back to Oakland – he simply shrieked that I "made Al" move the team. But he had absolutely no idea what I had advised Al on this or on any other topic. He never asked me, nor had I ever shared with him, my thoughts about the move or or the advice I provided Al. I know also that Al had not shared that information with him, as Al told me that he had never shared with anyone what advice and recommendation I had given him with respect to his decision to move the team back to Oakland or with respect to a number of other matters. Many people, including this owner, would have been very surprised if they knew what I had advised Al on any number of issues over the course of my career.

I know exactly where this owner got those ideas. I know exactly who told him that I "forced Al" to do things and that I was to blame for all of the Raiders' bad decisions and I know why this person did this. If this ranting owner was going to take this guy seriously, I thought, then good luck to him.

This person had for years asserted to the media, to league officials, and to officials with other clubs that I was responsible for all that ailed the Raiders. He thought that they kept his comments confidential, but they did not.

In fact, at one lunch break at a league meeting, while seated with a handful of people from the league office and a couple of other clubs, I learned that this was "a thing" and that people had been laughing about this for years. At this lunch, conversation had turned to world events and we were discussing some ongoing turmoil in another part of the world. A league executive at the table mused aloud – in a humorous tone – "How will (this club executive) blame this on Amy?" Everyone laughed, including me.

This small group owners' meeting was not, by the way, the first occasion on which I had heard that people thought that I controlled Al. There were a number of people from whom Al had distanced himself over the years who claimed I had forced him to do so. When Al distanced himself from people, he usually told me why. Sometimes I agreed with his reasoning, sometimes I did not. There were also instances in which I thought Al should (and wished he would) distance himself from people, when he did not. Al decided with whom he would or would not associate.

Similarly, there were a fair number of people who were angered by our business decisions who claimed that I dictated such decisions to Al. I recall one elected city official who accused me of controlling Al and dictating all of Al's decisions, all the while ranting and raving that he had never met anyone who was harder to influence or to sway.

There's an obvious and interesting intellectual inconsistency in all of this. Some of the very people who complained that Al could not be controlled also complained that I controlled him. Some of the very people who threw up their hands, distancing themselves from Al's decisions, asserting that they couldn't influence those decisions, accused me of making his decisions for him. To assert that I controlled Al was not only intellectually dishonest, it was absurd, but it happened often, most particularly when people did not want to accept that Al made decisions they didn't like.

All of that said, there were a lot of times that I wished I could control Al.

Ironically, there was an instance when Al accused me of "thought control," not of him, but of others. He accused me of inserting my doubts about and objections to our negotiating positions into the minds of those with whom we were negotiating. On this occasion, when articulating to Al my disagreement with a position he wanted me to take in a negotiation, he fired back: "There you go again; you think of these things and that puts them in their minds, they wouldn't think of them otherwise."

"Oh, I can mind meld...is that what you're suggesting?" I asked. "I must be pretty powerful," I added, thinking that there were plenty of times I wished I could "mind meld" him. Al responded, "Aw fuck," and hung up.

At the conclusion of the formal portion of the small group owner's meeting, those of us in attendance sat down for dinner in an adjacent room. I sensed that the dinner was strained, but I do not know if that was the sense of others in attendance.

After that dinner, I went to my hotel room and called Al to give him an update, as I often did after meetings. As I began telling him what happened, I started crying. I think it was because I was stunned by the level of intensity of the invective.

I wasn't horrified that I was crying. Neither was Al. I am strong and tough, yet I cried. Al is strong and tough, yet he didn't care that I cried. I wasn't embarrassed that I cried. Al wasn't bothered that I cried. It did not affect our relationship.

I cried on one other occasion during my career – also while on a phone call with Al. Al had directed two of us on staff to do something that I thought was idiotic and that quite obviously was going to be very hard to do.

Al had instructed us to articulate to an absolutely spectacular, tremendously respected broadcaster with the television network that would be broadcasting our upcoming game something that I thought was absurd and offensive. I tried everything I could to convince Al that this was a really bad idea. I told him it was dumb and that it would be to our decided detriment, but I couldn't convince him that we shouldn't do it.

Although Al had instructed two of us to deliver this message to this sensational broadcaster, my coworker disappeared when the moment to do so arose. He didn't tell Al that he wouldn't participate; he simply made himself scarce.

So I handled it. I shared Al's point of view. Of course, I didn't articulate that it was Al's view and I didn't blame Al. I stated the view as that of the organization and did so as diplomatically as I could. I tried to make the best of a wretched situation, but sometimes, when a position is ridiculous, any effort at diplomacy falls short.

When I was done, I went up to my office and I called Al, and I started crying. I cried because I was furious with him and with myself and with the whole situation.

Al told me that he felt badly and that it was his fault that this had happened. After we finished our conversation, and unbeknownst to me, Al called my husband and asked him to drive to the office, pick me up, and drive me home that night, explaining that he didn't believe I should drive myself home. He was worried.

I know this, because my husband called me in my office and said: "Al Davis just called me, he's worried about you, and he wants me to come pick you up and drive you home – he doesn't think you should drive yourself." I remember asking: "How did he get your office number?" My husband wondered the same. I later learned that Al asked one of my coworkers for it.

While Al felt badly that I was upset, he was not bothered that I cried, just as he wasn't in the instance after the small group owners meeting.

Decades later, I apologized to the tremendous broadcaster and gentleman to whom I addressed our remarks and he could not have been more gracious and understanding when I did.

I didn't share these stories about crying in a work environment because I believe that crying should be used as strategy in business or because I am proud that I cried. I did so because I believe they're instructive.

Common thought is that women must never cry on the job. We're told it is the worst thing that we can do, that it shows weakness and unsuitability for working in a "man's world." We're told that it shows that we can't handle pressure or the challenges of the business. We're told that women who cry in business won't succeed. And yet, in my case, this gender-based tautology was disproved.

On two occasions, I cried to a man (my boss and the controlling owner of the organization for which I worked) who was as strong and tough as anyone I have ever known or can imagine. This was a man who no one would believe would tolerate crying, who no one would believe would continue to work with someone who cried, and who no one would believe would support and promote someone who cried. But he wasn't bothered; he continued to work with me and to trust me, and and he promoted me. After all, when I cried in the first instance, I was not yet the organization's CEO. Clearly, my so doing did not dissuade Al from naming me as such, some years later.

He didn't care that I cried. He did care about me.

Al was incredibly unique.

(By way of note, on neither of the occasions on which I cried with Al did I cry nearly as hard as when I was watching *Free Willy*.)

OVER THE COURSE OF MY career, there were a few incidents in which employees cried to me, sometimes for reasons relating to work, sometimes for reasons relating to their personal lives. In each of those instances, the employee was male. I didn't enjoy those moments, but I did my best to act reasonably and honorably. It was the right thing to do for many reasons and it certainly would have been hypocritical if I were any less understanding and supportive than Al was with me.

And as to our conversation after the incident in the small group owners meeting – Al was magnificent. He could not have been kinder or more caring or more supportive. He was only concerned that I was okay. And I was. I was fine. Al was angry but his fury was directed at the owner who excoriated me. He noted that if anyone was to blame for the issues that bothered this owner, it was him (Al), not me. He remarked that I had been yelling at him about those same topics for years. Al made another interesting point: the owner who attacked me had never raised those issues with him – not once.

Al was incensed with this owner and called him a cocksucker a lot of times that night. (I don't know, though, whether he used one word or two.)

8

SHARIA LAW

ABOUT A MONTH OR SO AFTER THAT SMALL GROUP OWNERS meeting, I was in Al's office with him and two coworkers discussing some business issues. At one point, I had to leave the room for a moment in order to grab some financial documents from my office.

My coworkers, who had remained in Al's office while I ran to mine, later told me that while I was gone, Al again expressed how furious he was with this owner, and repeated that this owner had accosted me about issues that he never raised with him. Al also repeated that I'd argued with him about these issues for years. Clearly, this was still on Al's mind. They also told me that Al said: "Oh, fuck him, he wants Sharia law."

I didn't believe that this owner behaved as he did because I was a woman. I had seen him treat men who worked for other clubs and for the league office in a rough manner. I believe that he would have behaved in the same manner were I a man, which is as it should have been. After all, if gender neutrality is the goal, then women and men should be treated in the same manner, even when that manner is unpleasant. Quite a few people I respect have told me I shouldn't be so quick to give him the benefit of the doubt, but I did. That said, Al clearly believed that there was a link between this owner's behavior and my gender and he was angry.

It was just so wonderfully Al to intertwine an "Oh fuck him" with a reference to current world affairs in his strong defense of me. It really did touch me deeply. As one of my coworkers and I noted when discussing this later, Al was one of a kind.

AT SOME POINT MANY YEARS into my career, I saw a cartoon that made me think of my job and of Al, and laugh. The drawing depicted what appeared to be a husband and wife at the breakfast table. The man was reading a newspaper or journal which bore a bold headline proclaiming that stress at work was a leading cause of heart attacks.

The man looked up at his wife with an uncomprehending expression on his face and said, in what I imagined to be a quizzical tone, "I don't have stress at work." His wife responded, "No dear, you're a carrier."

On so many occasions after I saw that cartoon, I thought of it while interacting with Al. When the perfect opportunity arose, I explained the cartoon to him, and when I was done, he looked at me and said, "What's the point?" I responded, "No dear, you're a carrier." There were many occasions after that when I would look at him and simply say, "No dear, you're a carrier." He didn't laugh, but I did, every time.

AL SHOUTED AND SWORE AT most of the people who worked for him. The more closely one worked with Al, the more one experienced the shouting and swearing. But if someone outside of the organization criticized one of us, Al would vigorously defend us. On a few occasions when he was defending someone from external criticism, I loudly declared: "They can't do that to our pledges; only Al can do that to our pledges." I explained that I was paraphrasing *Animal House*. He looked at me uncomprehendingly and said, "Aw fuck."

AL PERIODICALLY NOTED THAT I spoke in a manner that didn't always resonate with him. He frequently said to me: "You know how you are with words." He often said to others: "You know how she is with words."

This arose in one instance in which two of our prominent players had filed grievances against the organization. Al didn't believe there was any merit to the grievances (Al never believed there was any merit to any of the claims ever asserted against the Raiders) and when a few of us met to discuss them, Al shared his view on how we would defend ourselves. After listening to his explanation, I told him that his argument was circular.

He told me that he didn't understand what I meant when I said his argument was circular. Actually, what he said was: "I don't know what the fuck you're talking about." He then looked to another person who was in the room and said: "I don't understand her, do you understand her? You know how she is with words."

I again attempted to explain to him why his argument was circular. I failed. I could not convince him that his argument was circular and for that matter, I was unable to define "circular argument" to his satisfaction. For weeks, as were preparing for the hearing on these grievances, I tried to explain this in different ways. I got nowhere. As the date for the grievance hearing approached, Harold Henderson, who was then the league's executive vice president for labor relations, called Al to discuss these grievances.

After Al finished his conversation with Harold, he called me into his office. "Harold says it's circular," Al told me.

I stood there and stared at him. I didn't move. I didn't say anything. I just stood there and stared at him. Finally, I said, "Well, if Harold says it's circular, then it must be circular." I then walked out. To this day, anytime someone states the obvious or something we already know, my husband and I laughingly say: "Thanks, Harold."

THE JOB HAD OODLES OF challenges – there were many warm and wonderful moments, but the challenges were significant.

Perhaps the biggest challenge I faced over the course of my entire career with the Raiders was that I was not permitted to fire those employees who predated me in the organization – and there were quite a few of them. As I grew and grew up and advanced within the organization, many of those employees were to report to me – in theory, that is. They knew that I had no authority to terminate them, affect the terms of their employment, or hold them accountable for their performance. They believed Al would insulate and protect them, and they were right; he did.

Not too long after I was hired, Al directed me to inform a senior employee – considerably more senior than I – that at the end of each day he was to provide me with a detailed accounting of how he had spent every hour that day. Al was quite specific. He told me what he wanted the sheet to look like – it was to be an hour-by-hour grid. The employee in question was to fill it in and provide it to me before he left each day. I told Al that this was a really bad idea for many reasons. I told him that I would prefer to work with this employee to improve his productivity and accountability rather than to act as his prison guard or a really lousy elementary school teacher. Al was unwavering. So I then told him that if he wanted this done, that he should do this. Again, Al was unmoved.

And so, when this employee learned that at the end of each day he was to provide me a sheet detailing his activities of the day on an hour-by-hour basis before he went home, he did just that. He handed me a sheet of paper – it bore that day's date – and it had a big, bold note: MYOFB. I remembered that acronym from elementary school: mind your own fucking business. Yeah, this would go well.

I was in a leadership role at a young age, I was learning to lead and I was trying to lead people who knew I had no authority whatsoever to hold them accountable, to impact their terms of employment, or to terminate them. It was a challenge.

For decades, much has been said and written about the need to change the Raiders' "locker room culture." I too thought that certain significant changes needed to be made throughout the organization, and not just with respect to locker room culture. The changes that I believed needed to be made transcended the locker room; they permeated the organization.

I often shared with Al my strongly held views about the changes I believed were necessary. He did not agree and in fact, periodically implored me to stop raising the subject, stating that I could make those changes when he wasn't here anymore. (It was clear that "not here anymore" meant after he had passed away.)

Likewise, there were instances in which I suggested to Al that we terminate some longtime employees, as I did not believe that they were serving the organization well for any number of reasons. While Al often agreed with me that there were good reasons for those suggested terminations, with one exception (in which there were serious extenuating circumstances), he would not allow me to terminate these employees. Instead, he'd simply say, "Someday they'll get a big surprise." Only they never did.

Organizational culture is fascinating in many respects. Many football organizations – certainly the Raiders – retain employees for decades upon decades. In the case of the Raiders, although Al is gone, there still remain within the organization individuals who have been with the team since well before I joined it and others who have been with the team for what in employment terms is an eternity.

Whether and how an organization chooses to balance its desire to be loyal with the need to evolve and grow is a fascinating issue. I think it is possible to achieve a good balance in that regard. Al chose not to strive for balance and instead prioritized loyalty to the exclusion of all else, even in instances in which I believed that I had offered compelling arguments that such loyalty was unwarranted. That was Al's decision to make, of course. He believed strongly in a method of doing business that had worked well for him for many years and he was unwilling to make significant changes during his lifetime. I know that I exasperated him by continually urging him to do so – he told me that I did (in less polite terms). Al wanted to do it his way, as he and Frank Sinatra crooned.

WHEN AL ENDED A PHONE conversation, most of the time he did so without saying goodbye or otherwise signaling that he was done conversing. He simply hung up. No goodbye. Just click. When Al was done, he was done.

I don't know when it happened, but a number of years into my career, I realized that somewhere along the line, I adopted this practice. I would be speaking with someone – it could be a coworker, a league-office employee, a business associate – heck, it could be my husband, my father, a sibling, a friend – and when from my perspective, the conversation had run its useful course, I simply hung up. No goodbye, just click. I think I may still do this. I learned and adopted a lot of behavior from Al. Some good, some not so good.

I SPENT A LOT OF time with Al when he came off of the practice field in the very late afternoon or early evening. This was when we had so many of our substantive, thoughtful discussions. I would wait for practice to end, wait for him to leave the field, wait for him to speak with football personnel on the way in, and wait for him to make his way to his office. Once he was there, I joined him and we sat in two chairs facing a large television. Soon, someone would bring him the film or the tape of practice (of course, it hadn't been film or tape for years – but we still called it film or tape).

As we sat together watching practice, I updated him, answered his questions, sought his input, obtained his signature on documents, and discussed a wide variety of league and Raiders matters. Periodically, football personnel – trainers, scouts, and coaches – would drop in and provide him with reports and updates he requested. I learned a lot as I listened to those conversations.

Al liked chocolate. As we sat together, he would often call to one of his assistants, asking her to bring him some chocolate and a diet cola, which he simply called "a diet." "Bring me a diet," he called to an assistant. "Can I have some chocolate?" he often added. Sometimes, he was more specific: "Bring me a Twinx." Twinx meant Twix. Al always offered to share his chocolate with me, whether it was a "Twinx" or something else.

These hours after practice were the best time to discuss all sorts of business, issues, financial and banking matters, employee issues, legal issues, league matters, profit and loss projections – really, all topics. I would come prepared with a list of things to discuss and documents for Al to sign. As I tried to address these matters, Al would frequently interrupt me and say, "Shhh, wait a minute." I can hear his voice now: "Shhh, wait a minute." I must have heard those words – "Shhh, wait a minute" – in that context millions of times over the decades.

To this day, when I am focused and do not want to be interrupted, I say, "Shhh, wait a minute" to whomever is interrupting me. I think of Al as I do so, and I smile warmly. The people to whom I say, "Shhh, wait a minute" do not.

Often, as we sat together and as I was trying to get him to focus on business while he was watching practice, he'd say, "Did you see that?" I never did figure out whether he was testing me or whether he simply wanted to know if I saw something he'd seen. Of course I was watching, and I responded accordingly, "Yes, I saw that," and I'd explain what I saw.

"Yes, I saw the linebacker got sucked inside…now will you sign the document?"

"Shhh, wait a minute."

I LEARNED SO MUCH ABOUT football when discussing practice and games with Al. He shared his observations with me and he patiently answered all of my questions. "Why don't we send extra men, instead of just rushing four?" I asked. "Can he handle him, or will he need help (blocking)?" I asked about a particular matchup in our upcoming game. "Can he cover him or will he need help?" I queried.

Al also firmly let me know that I was not a coach. "Were I the defensive coordinator…." I would say.

"…You're not," he would respond. But Al taught me a lot about football. I always understood what a privilege that was – to learn football from Al Davis.

"The quarterback must go down, and he must go down hard," Al would often tell me.

As much as Al emphasized the need to pressure the passer, he felt strongly that we should do so with our defensive front alone and he resisted the idea of sending extra men. He explained to me why he resisted the concept of sending extra men, why he was reluctant to blitz, and why he believed that pressure could and should be achieved using only our defensive front. "That's fine if it works," I replied, "but then it better work." On occasion, when we were having trouble getting to the quarterback, I would ask, "How about if we send extra men?" knowing it would annoy him.

Al spent more time discussing football with me than many would have expected.

Unrelated to our conversation about blitzes, Al periodically reminded me about the importance of corners. One occasion on which he did so was after Art Shell's first game as head coach in 1989. We played the Jets on *Monday Night Football* in New York and we abused their corners. When we spoke the morning after the game, Al again reminded me, "Never leave a team without corners, kid."

Over the course of my career, a number of people told me that they initially assumed that I was a businessperson who just happened to be in football, and that they were surprised to learn of my passion for the game and that I knew Xs and Os and matchups – that I knew football.

I never considered myself a businessperson who just happened to work in football; I considered myself a football person whose contribution to the organization would be in business milieu.

I have loved football since I was in the seventh grade. I didn't grow up in a family of avid football fans; my parents would host or join a Super Bowl party every year, but that was it. My family didn't go to or watch football games on the weekends – they certainly never planned their weekends around football. My parents wanted all of us to be outside in the fresh air; I preferred to stay home and watch football.

A few times, my holiday gift to my father was tickets to a Los Angeles Rams game (this, of course, was in the years before the Raiders moved to Los Angeles). He was happy because it was time spent together, and I got to go to a football game. I had a wonderful friend who was a fullback during our years together at Cal and he taught me a lot about the nuances of the game. A few years after I joined the Raiders, I got in touch with him to tease him about the fact that that I periodically reverted to assessing both sides of the line of scrimmage through the eyes of a fullback. Of course, looking at things from through the eyes of a fullback does provide an interesting perspective on the game.

Even if I didn't love football, I would have learned it, just as if had I worked for a lumberyard, I would have learned everything I could about lumber. But I did love and understand football before I joined the organization.

Of course, my knowledge grew over the course of my career. After all, I had the incredible privilege of sitting beside Al Davis for almost three decades, learning the game from him.

One of the things I love about football is that it is highly cerebral. The first time I saw a game, I decided that it was like a game of chess, played by very large, very strong, very fast men. It is a game of matchups in which one must find ways to exploit the weaknesses of an opponent while camouflaging, to the extent possible, the weaknesses of one's own team. How do our backs match up against your linebackers? How does our offensive line match up against your defensive line? Do we need to send extra men? Do we need to keep extra men in to block? Can our corners cover your receivers man to man? Should we play zone?

The best coaches exploit matchups and hide deficiencies to prevent other coaches from so doing. The best coaches maximize the talent on their roster, positioning players to succeed. The worst coaches insist on forcing players into their system, irrespective of whether the players are suited for it. It never ceases to amaze me when coaches do that.

If your quarterback is a pure, drop-back, pocket passer who is not mobile, why would you implement a system or scheme predicated on quarterback mobility and movement? That's dumb. If you have a solid or potentially explosive running back who has met with his best success behind a power-blocking scheme, why would you put in a zone-blocking scheme? That's dumb. Why would you take dominating pass rushers and place them in a scheme in which they drop back into coverage the majority of the plays? That's dumb.

If a choir director asks an alto to sing soprano, he or she shouldn't be surprised when the music doesn't sound good.

I understand that coaches want players who will fit their systems – and in an ideal world, that's great. But that isn't always possible, particularly when a coach initially joins an organization and a roster is already in place. So instead of taking square pegs and trying to force them into round holes, good coaches design and implement systems around the players they have and put those players in the best position to succeed – the best position to win.

I ALSO HAVE DISDAIN FOR what I refer to as the "my guy mantra." So often, when general managers are hired, they talk about "my guy." They say: "I want my guy," "I gotta get my guy," or "I got my guy."

"My guy" is often used by general managers to refer to a coach. Okay, that makes sense and in a perfect world, a general manager should be able to bring in a coach. But you know what? Sometimes that's not possible and sometimes, it's not optimal, especially in the first year of a general manager's tenure, when he may have been hired after all of the best coaches are off the market. And you know what? Having the best guy is more important than having your guy. Were I hired as the general manager of a team for which Bill Belichick was the coach, guess what – he's my guy. If you have the best guy in place, spend your energy finding a way to way to work together. In other words, grow up. Find a way to work with the best people possible, irrespective of whether you hired them or not.

On one occasion on which we were looking to hire a new coach Al allowed me to participate. He asked me to spend time with some candidates and after I did, he asked me which of them I would hire. Without hesitation, I said Bill Belichick. (This was before Bill went to New England.) Al didn't hire Bill, but he did hire another very good coach.

Over the years, as Bill went on to have tremendous success, Al periodically said to me: "You know how to pick a coach, kid."

I thought that my recommendation of Bill would remain between Al and me and that no one would ever know of it. Then, many years later, when Al was interacting with the media at the conclusion of a press conference, he told the assembled writers that I had told him to hire Belichick. I was stunned that he shared that. Stunned, but very happy. And I was pleased that one writer included that information in a story.

There were a number of reasons I recommended that we hire Bill. One was his obvious intelligence. I have always believed that intelligence matters and throughout my career I observed this was the case in football just as it was in business in general.

Someone I respect recently said of Bill Belichick: "He is wicked smart." Exactly. He is one of the smartest football men I have ever known or known of. I believe that he is, to date, the best football coach of all time. Bill maximizes the talent on his roster, he exploits matchups, he disguises deficiencies, he does everything possible to put his players and his teams in the best position to win, and he does so extraordinarily well.

While on the topic of coaches and coaching intelligence, I'll note something else that has always perplexed – and infuriated – me: when coaches stop doing something that is working. Time and again I have seen coaches change course during a game, even when what they were doing was effective. Running game is working – okay, let's stop running. Deep passing game is working – okay, let's shift to screen passes and quick, short outs. If something is working, make the defense take it away. If a team can't stop what you are doing, why in the world would you make their job easy for them and stop it yourself? It always strikes me that when coaches do this, they are trying to demonstrate that they are smart. But it's not smart. Smart coaches make a defense take something away; they don't do it for them. Don't try to look smart. And don't be cute. I can't stand when coaches get cute in a game. Position your team to win.

JUST AS I WAS NOT a coach, as Al liked to remind me, I was obviously not a player. Although, as a coworker once said when the team was struggling on special teams: "If we put Amy in, at least she'll try to slow someone down by holding."

I have been asked what position I would have liked to have played were I a man, with the physique and talent to play any position. I would have wanted to be a defensive end (in a 4-3 scheme), a dominant pass rusher who excelled in third-down passing situations. My second choice would be to play strong safety, as I could roam the middle of the field and hit people.

I wasn't a coach or a player, but I loved occasions on which I was able to make a direct, on-field contribution on game day.

During one home game, one of our players who was inactive due to injury, and was therefore in street clothes, entered a fight from the sideline. After the fight had been broken up and play had resumed, the league observer who was in the press box asked a few of us to identify that player. I refused to answer and implored others not to do so. After all, we were hopeful he would be ready to go the next week, and I didn't want him suspended for a game or games. The league official stormed over to a Raiders executive and demanded that I be ejected from the press box. I thought I might be kicked out. The Raiders executive looked at me, looked at him, looked back at me, and then instead of ejecting or admonishing me, yanked the league official's credential off his belt loop, which elated me. I was a Raider.

Another time, during pregame warm-ups in 2011, an assistant coach ran up to me on the sideline, where I was entertaining the organization's sponsors, suite holders, business partners, and others. "Coach sent me to get you," he said. "We have a problem."

The problem was that the referee had explained to our kicker and to this assistant coach that for field-goal tries, we would have to place the ball about an inch from where we wished and believed we were permitted to place it. That inch made a huge difference that day because the game was during the baseball season, so a significant portion of the football field was a dirt infield. If we moved the ball the inch we were instructed to move it, a field goal try on one end of the field would be off the dirt. Our kicker, Sebastian Janikowski, was agitated and wanted the ball placed on the grass, not the dirt.

I called the league office, explained the situation, and stated that I thought that the referee was wrong. The league executive on the phone agreed with my interpretation of the rule. "Hold tight," he said.

He then contacted the league observer of officials, who was in the press box, and instructed him to go find me on the field. When he found me, I again explained our understanding of the rule and he too agreed that we should be allowed to place the ball where we believed it could (and should) be placed. Sebastian thanked me, which felt good. We won that day. I have no idea whatsoever whether my involvement made one bit of difference – it probably didn't. I certainly like to amuse myself by believing that I contributed in a direct manner to that victory, but Sebastian could have kicked it from 60 yards off the dirt standing on his head.

Another way in which I involved myself in football matters on game day involved officiating. Whenever I observed what I believed to be a call against us that should not have been made, or the absence of a call against our opponent which should have been made, I immediately emailed Mike Pereira, the league executive who oversaw the officiating department, who was in the league command center in New York. Much to Al's chagrin, Mike and I were friends. "How's your friend, that fuckin' Mike Pereira," Al would often ask. He wasn't teasing; he didn't understand why – and he was annoyed that – I was friends with Mike. If I didn't receive an immediate response from "that fuckin' Mike Pereira," I would keep hitting resend (again and again and again) until I did. Mike shared with me that whenever he saw (or someone else in the command center called to his attention) a call or a noncall in our game that he believed would make me angry, he started counting aloud, backward from ten, to see how long it would take until he received my email. He said he never got close to one. Mike and I laughed about this then and we laugh about it to this day. Did any of this do us any good? No. But it didn't harm us, he assured me. And I felt it important to point out to him every wrong call in one of our games, noting to him that this was almost a full-time job.

I am not a conspiracy theorist. Well, I am convinced that there was more than one shooter that day in Dallas (the laws of physics and aerodynamics, among other things, suggest that there was). That instance aside, I am not a conspiracy theorist. But it certainly seemed to me that there were a disproportionate number of bad calls and bad noncalls in our games. Conclude what you'd like.

I started my game-day habit of emailing Mike (and emailing and emailing and emailing him) the season we met. That meeting occurred when Mike visited our facility in the spring or early summer to meet with our coaches to go over rule changes and points of emphasis for the upcoming season. I knew that Mike was scheduled to be in our offices, so I asked the assistant to the head coach to tell him that I wished to spend a few moments with him before he left. I wanted to discuss illegal contact – more precisely, I wanted to discuss what I perceived to be the very inconsistent interpretation and application of illegal-contact rules. As Mike would later tell the story, when he was told that I wanted to see him, he was surprised and expected the worst. He came into my office and we had what we both would later agree was a terrific discussion about the application of the illegal-contact rules.

That initial meeting marked the beginning of what many people in the league referred to as an unlikely friendship. Al was, as noted, more succinct: "Your friend, that fuckin' Mike Pereira."

Notwithstanding that I liked Mike, I sure did yell at him a lot about what I believed to be bad calls made against us and what I believed to be noncalls that should have been made against our opponents. We once had a huge blow-up – okay, I had a huge blow-up – over a letter Mike sent to me. Every day, teams receive what is referred to as a "pouch" from the league office. That pouch is a single package or a box containing correspondence for many people with the club. One day, the pouch contained a letter to me from Mike. While it wasn't unusual for me to receive correspondence from him (memoranda to all club executives, copies of letters to coaches, explanations of rules and interpretations thereof), this correspondence struck me as a bit odd, as it appeared to be both personal and formal. The letter was in one of the league's nice envelopes, on good stationery, and it was addressed to me; it was not something that was circulated to a group of people. My initial reaction (that this was odd) soon gave way to another reaction: fury. I was livid; I was enraged; I was so mad I was almost apoplectic.

Mike's letter reminded me of the sort of letter a teacher or the principal of one's school sends to the parents of a misbehaving student. (I was quite familiar with those.) In the letter, Mike explained that it had been called to his attention that my game-day interaction with a league observer was inappropriate and offensive. He admonished me for my behavior and instructed me to behave more appropriately and, in particular, to watch my language. His letter stated that it had been suggested to him that he should fine me for my behavior, but that he was instead issuing this warning. I was seething. I picked up the phone and called Mike and told him that his letter was the most obnoxious, offensive, infuriating letter I had ever received – and I noted that I had received some doozies in the past. I told him that it reminded me of a "bad notice" sent by a teacher or a principal, mumbling that I had some experience with those. (I am confident that Mike was not surprised that I had.) I shouted that he should never again send me "another fucking letter like that" and that he should just fine me instead. He let me rant. I thought I heard him chuckle a little and that made me even madder, so I went on and again told him not to send "another fucking letter like that" ever again and to just fine me and I hung up. Mike's job was such that coaches, general managers, and team executives called him and ranted all the time. I don't know where on the rant-o-meter he ranked my call, but I think, and I hope, it was high.

When I recounted that story to my husband that night, he too allowed me to rant. After I was done, he said, "How about if you just let him send you letters and don't ask to be fined?"

Even after I received that letter, I continued to email (and email and email and email) Mike on game day. And even though Al always referred to him as "your friend, that fuckin' Mike Pereira," we remained (and still are) friends.

9
TO THINE OWN
SELF BE TRUE

AS FOCUS ON A LINKAGE BETWEEN BRAIN INJURIES AND SPORTS (football in particular) has increased, I am frequently asked whether, if I had a son, I would want him to play football. This is not an easy question for me. I do not know what my answer would be, and since I do not have a son, I have not been forced to reach a conclusion.

Putting aside the issue of football, I am a worrywart when it comes to people I love. The magnitude of my worry – and my vivid imagination about the harm that may befall those I love – is a running joke among my family, friends, and colleagues. If someone is not where I believe he or she should be at the time I believe he or she should be there, I am poised and ready to call (and have in fact called) the authorities to request a search of roads and hospitals. You're late for a meeting? Obviously, you must have driven off the side of the road and need my help. You're not where you're supposed to be? You must have been kidnapped and need my help. Those are not exaggerations.

I once concluded that a team executive who was late for a meeting must have driven into a ditch, and I mobilized a squadron of people to find him.

I'd been with the organization only a short time when I concluded that Al had been kidnapped.

Many evenings after most people had gone home, often when it was dark, Al would go out to the practice fields and jog. I always knew that even if I couldn't catch him after practice to discuss something, I could wait until after he finished jogging, and catch him when he returned. Those were quiet, relaxed times when I could interact with him.

One night, I went to find him in his office after I thought he should have been back inside, but he wasn't there. I went back to my office, waited a bit, checked back periodically, but still no Al. It seemed to me that he had been out back longer than usual so I became worried. I waited just a bit longer and then went out to the fields to find him. He wasn't there. Okay, he wasn't in his office and he wasn't on the fields or any place in between. Now, I was really worried. I checked everywhere in the building that housed our business operations but couldn't find him. I called the building that housed our football operations and was told that he wasn't there. Now, I was really panicked.

One of Al's assistants knew that I was looking for him everywhere. I found her and said: "Al's been kidnapped." The expression on her face suggested that she thought I was nuts, but my worry affected her and she too became worried. She helped me look for Al, we couldn't find him. We were in the process of placing a call to the local police department when he walked out of the shower area in the back of his office and toward his desk. "You're alive! You're alive!" I shouted. "You haven't been kidnapped," I exclaimed, "you're here, you're alive." He looked at me like I was insane. Perhaps, though, this suggested to him that I cared and that I would look out for him and come to his aid if ever I believed harm had befallen him.

I DON'T KNOW WHETHER AL was more bemused when I convinced myself that he was kidnapped or when I walked into his office dressed as a cat. It was early evening and we were set to host a Halloween party for a large group of children who lived in an area in which it was not safe to trick or treat. I was wearing a black sweater and black pants, to which I had pinned a long fuzzy tail. I had black fuzzy ears on my head and I had drawn a cat nose on mine and whiskers on my face. It was a Halloween party; of course I dressed up. Just as I was heading downstairs to greet the kids, Al called out for me to come to his office. I walked in, answered the questions he posed, engaged in a very substantive discussion about the topics he raised, and left. As I was walking out, I heard Al call out to one of his assistants, "What the fuck was that?" "She's dressed as a cat, Mr. Davis," I heard the assistant call back. "A cat," he responded in a bewildered tone. "She's dressed as a fuckin' cat."

SOME OF THE VERY BEST advice I have received in life was provided by my parents. Of course, I didn't realize at the time they shared this advice that it was so valuable, and I rolled my eyes a lot.

From the time I can remember, my mother counseled me: to thine own self be true. It wasn't until I was an adult that I realized that my mother was quoting Polonius, who shared that advice with Laertes in *Hamlet*. My mother or Polonius, it's spectacular advice: to thine own self be true. It is the best advice I have ever received.

"A job worth doing is a job worth doing well," my parents frequently told me, mostly when I wasn't doing something well.

"If you're gonna do it, do it right," was another mantra I heard a lot, mostly when I wasn't doing something right. When I heard those admonitions as a child and as a teen, I would get mad. I realized many years later that this advice served me well.

My parents constantly emphasized the importance of finding something I loved to do and doing it with all my heart. My parents would not have cared one bit what I chose to do – what I earned or what I accomplished – as long as I loved what I did. I did find something I loved, and I did it with all my heart.

Another piece of advice that still resonates: the world doesn't owe you a living. That's true; the world owes none of us a living. We're not entitled to anything.

Another good nugget: anticipate – don't wait until you are asked to do something, do it before you are asked.

Also very valuable: never compare what you have with what others have.

While I can't recall my parents ever specifically telling me that attention to detail is important, I am certain that observing their attention to detail influenced me. Attention to detail matters.

If I were asked to single out the best, most important, and most valuable words of advice I ever received it would be those that my mother (and Polonius) shared: to thine own self be true.

Al was certainly true to himself. Even when I disagreed with his decisions and his behavior, I admired (sometimes begrudgingly) his refusal to let anyone dictate his beliefs.

THERE ARE MANY URBAN LEGENDS about Al and the Raiders. Throughout my career I bristled when anyone said "Al always does *x*" or "Al never does *y*" or "Al thinks" or "Al believes." I still bristle when I hear such things. Those proclamations were – and are – most often wrong.

From the moment I joined the Raiders, I was told more times than I can count, "Al won't let us do this" or "Al won't let us do that," but I can count on one hand (with fingers to spare) the times that these proclamations were right.

Just a few years into my career, well before I had any authority to do so, I decided to call a staff meeting. I don't know what prompted me to do so, other than I thought that a staff meeting would be a good idea. In the relatively brief time I had been with the club, there had been no staff meetings for business operations personnel and I thought that one would be beneficial. Years later, when I reflected upon my decision to call this meeting, I realized how odd that was and why so many employees found it disconcerting. Who the hell was I to call a staff meeting? But I thought there should be one, so I called it.

"Al doesn't allow staff meetings," I was told. "When Al hears about this, he's gonna be pissed," I heard. "If Al hears about this, he'll cancel it,"

I was cautioned. Well, we had that staff meeting, and when I spoke with Al on an unrelated matter later that day, he very casually asked how the meeting went. The very relaxed manner in which he asked me that told me two things: (a) he had been alerted to the fact that I had called a staff meeting; and (b) he wasn't at all bothered that I had done so. After all, he wasn't shy – if he was bothered, he would have let me know that he was, in no uncertain terms.

Even before I called that staff meeting, I had started trying to learn as much as I could about everything. I did so because I was thrilled to be part of the organization and it was natural for me to want to learn everything I could about it, not because I was looking to advance or for any other reason.

Our offices in Los Angeles were in a former middle school that had been closed by the school district. I wandered through the complex. I walked into what had been the principal's office, which the organization had converted into the ticket office, and asked all sorts of questions about attendance, seating, pricing, and supply and demand. On Saturdays before home games, I alphabetized the will call envelopes. I walked into the public relations, marketing, merchandise, scouting, finance, and other departments and did the same. I asked a lot of questions.

It never occurred to me at the time that my coworkers would be or were bothered by my inquisitiveness. I was interested and I was trying to learn all that I could. It never struck me that what I was doing was anything but normal. It never occurred to me that all employees of a business wouldn't want to and try to learn all that they could about the business for which they worked. I realized many years later that my interest and inquisitiveness were seen as nosy and intrusive and that I was perceived as encroaching into areas "belonging" to others. I annoyed and offended a lot of people.

As I listened and learned, it struck me that employees operated in silos, were extraordinarily territorial with respect to their fiefdoms, and were tremendously proprietary with information.

Many employees rebuked me as I walked through the buildings asking questions and told me that my doing so would make Al mad. "Al doesn't like people asking questions," I was told. "Al doesn't like people butting into things," I heard. "Al won't like you snooping," I was counseled. "Al wants everyone to mind their own business," I heard repeatedly.

One day, though, I ran into Al as he was walking downstairs while I was walking up. He paused on the staircase and asked me the status of ticket sales for our upcoming game. He wasn't angry – he simply asked me about the ticket count. Again, that told me two things: (a) he had been told of my inquiries, my interest, my roaming, and my probing; and (b) he wasn't bothered. I realized something else: know the answer. In this instance, I did, and I told him the status of ticket sales as of that day for the upcoming game.

Al did nothing to discourage my exploration and inquisitiveness. In fact, the manner in which he interacted with me encouraged me.

I learned more than facts as I roamed and probed and listened and assessed and I concluded that the way the Raiders operated at that time was not the way I believed a business should operate.

AL ALSO DIDN'T HAVE A problem with something else a bit unusual that I did early in my career.

Apollo 13 is one of my all-time favorite movies. Even though we all knew how the movie would end, I was captivated. When the NASA technicians dumped onto a conference table around which NASA engineers were gathered only the equipment and tools that the astronauts had with them in space, and the flight director instructed those engineers that they had to solve the problem using only those items, I was enthralled. When he explained that he wasn't concerned with what something was designed to do but, rather, what it could do, I was excited. When the director of NASA told him that could be the worst disaster NASA ever faced, and he replied, "We've never lost an American in space, we're sure as hell not gonna lose one on my watch," I was covered in goose bumps, as I am now.

That night, after I saw the movie, I checked the listings to see what time it was playing the next day at the theater complex near our offices. The next morning (I think it was a Monday), I eagerly zoomed through the business operations area of the facility, and announced to everyone I could find that there would be a field trip that day and I strongly encouraged everyone to attend. Tickets and snacks on the Raiders! There was no email, Facebook, Twitter, Instagram, Snapchat, or other method by which I could quickly communicate information about the proposed field trip to everyone, so I located everyone I could and extended this invitation in person. I suppose I could have found the old middle school public address system and figured out if and how it worked – but even if I found it, and even if it worked, an announcement would have carried to our football operations areas and that might have resulted in the cancellation of the field trip.

I was so excited. I wanted as many people as were able to do so to go on this field trip. I explained to everyone that I wanted to stay back, answer phones, and do anything and everything that I could to cover in their absence so that they could attend.

As I started zipping in and out of all the offices explaining this, I received some strange looks that suggested to me that people thought I was nuts. Maybe I was. I wasn't the CEO at the time; I was the junior attorney on staff. I had no authority to authorize a field trip and yet I was darting through the building telling everyone about it. I also had no authority to authorize the expenses associated with the field trip, but I did (popcorn and snacks included).

Many employees happily embarked upon the field trip; others did not. While the field trip was in progress, Al called in and asked to speak with one or two people who were at the movie. When he was told by someone who stayed back why those people weren't in the office, where they were, and how this came to be, he asked to speak with me. I didn't know what to expect when I was told that Al was on the phone and that he had been looking for people who were at the movie. I told him that I authorized a field trip and that I had also authorized the expenditure for it. I told him about the movie and the scenes described above and that I thought it important that everyone see such a powerful depiction of the success that can be achieved through commitment and teamwork. Al responded he thought he'd like that movie and that was that. He wasn't mad – not even about the authorization for popcorn and snacks.

OVER THE COURSE OF MY career, I interacted with many people in football – people with the Raiders and people with other teams – who didn't believe that all employees of an organization should work together. In fact, they believed that there should be a wall (they actually called it that: a wall) between football and business operations. That's dumb for many reasons.

To those who asserted that there should be a wall to keep business-people out of football, I replied that each and every area of the organization touches upon and interconnects with the others. The organization would be better and stronger, I stressed, if everyone communicated, cooperated, coordinated, and collaborated. I repeated my strongly held beliefs that those four words are fundamental to success as often as I did for a number of reasons, one of which was this: this wasn't the business ethos of the organization when I joined it.

Look, I'm not suggesting that the CPA decide whether to install a 3–4 or a 4–3 defense or that the chief revenue officer install goal-line packages. I'm not suggesting that the director of community relations decide whether to play a single high safety or that the social media director determine the 53-man roster. I am, however, suggesting that everyone in the organization should communicate, cooperate, coordinate, and collaborate.

Many who espouse the "build a wall between football and business" philosophy began their careers in football in a different era and don't understand that the league today is not what it was years ago. Others simply like the "build a wall" philosophy, irrespective of when they began working in football.

In my efforts to convince those who trumpeted the wall approach to business that not only would no harm come of having no wall, but the absence of a wall could lead to greater success, I pointed out that some of the very best football organizations of recent decades, the ones that consistently performed on the field at an extremely high level, eschew the wall concept and have instead created an integrated, synergistic, collaborative environment. I don't love the word *synergy*, perhaps because it is overused. I love the concept, I just don't love the word. The expression I like, and that I regularly use, is cross-pollination. The best businesses make sure that all departments, all employees, cross-pollinate.

It is also important to recognize that great ideas can come from anyone: the receptionist might have a terrific ticket sales idea; the youngest, newest assistant in the equipment room might have an excellent idea for the website; the strength coach might have a great idea for social media. No one has a monopoly on all the good ideas; no one has a monopoly on creativity. Everyone in the organization is important and should feel welcome – indeed, encouraged – to contribute.

Good businesses cultivate an environment in which everyone understands that credit doesn't matter. Good leaders don't take credit, they credit others. Good leaders don't assign blame; they accept it. As John F. Kennedy said, "Victory has a thousand fathers, but defeat is an orphan." That observation has been made about football games and the same can be said about ideas. Many claim credit for a good one, but a bad one? That baby is an orphan.

During my career, I saw credit taken and blame assigned many times. During my first season with the team, a coworker shared with me his astute observation of many a coach's behavior after a game: *I confess, he did it*. It was only years later that I understood how prevalent that approach was not only on the field, but off.

No one should fear that he or she – or an idea he or she offers – will be mocked. In a good environment, when an idea is shared, it sparks creative discourse. A discussion about the goofiest of ideas may produce the next brilliant one.

Just as employees should understand that it is okay to suggest a goofy idea, they should understand that it is okay to make mistakes. If people are afraid to make mistakes, they won't try to innovate or create, as they will be scared to experiment and explore. Not much that is new or exciting is generated in environments in which people are scared to make mistakes. Mistakes happen when people are trying to accomplish new things and to improve.

Not too long after I joined the Raiders, someone I met while working on a business transaction told me that he believed that the only people who don't make mistakes are those who don't try to accomplish anything. I think that is a wise observation.

I tried my best to convey that we would all make mistakes, and that when any one of us made a mistake, we would all work to fix it together. I emphasized that I would make mistakes and that I would count on my teammates to help me fix the mistakes I made, just as I would always do my best to help to fix mistakes they made. I find it easy to admit when I've make a mistake, and I find it easy to ask others for assistance. There were instances in which I gathered together a group of employees, explained that I had made a mistake, and asked them to help me fix it and together, we did.

In some instances, mistakes are harder to fix than in others, and in other instances, mistakes can't be fixed. I shared with my coworkers that my brother and sister-in-law are doctors, and if one of them shouted, "Oh, fuck!" during a procedure, that could signal a really big problem. I shared that I once had the tremendous privilege of taking a ride in an F-16 and if the pilot had screamed, "Oh, fuck!" while we were traveling at a tremendous speed, at a high altitude, upside down, that too could signal a really big problem. My point was, I told them, that as a general rule, business mistakes can be fixed or their impact mitigated.

The only mistake for which I had very little (if any) tolerance was a failure to communicate, cooperate, coordinate, and collaborate.

It is also important that every employee understand and believe that his or her job matters. If someone on the maintenance staff doesn't do his or her job well and leaves a slippery spot in the shower, and the starting left corner slips and tears an ACL, that employee didn't help us win. If the receptionist doesn't do his or her job well and misses a call from the agent of a free agent and a player we would have signed to improve our team thus signed with another team, that employee didn't help us win. If someone on the grounds crew doesn't do his or her job well and fails to fix a clump of grass or a divot on the practice field and the starting left tackle catches a cleat and tears an ACL, then that employee didn't help us win.

Every job is important, every employee has a role in helping the team win, and it is important to cultivate an environment in which everyone understands that he or she is important to success.

I RECEIVED MANY WORDS OF advice as I grew and advanced within the organization. Some of that advice came from executives and owners of other teams and some came from executives in the league office. Some was terrible.

Two people offered me this suggestion: seal off Al from every other Raiders employee – build a moat around him – and make sure that no one can get to him without going through you. One of the people who offered me that advice was his organization's most senior employee (its president) and he explained that this is how he structured his organization. The other person who offered me that advice was a team owner.

The president and CEO of another club explained to me that I must structure the organization such that there could be only one star: me.

I appreciated the fact that these men cared enough to offer me advice, and I know that they offered me words that they believed to be wise, but I disagreed with every bit of it. Those suggestions were – and are – antithetical to all of my beliefs about what constitutes a good business structure and environment.

I wanted all employees to have access to and to interact with Al.

I wanted all employees to shine as brightly as they could.

I believe the best businesses create and foster environments in which everyone is able and encouraged not only to succeed, but to shine. After all, an organization full of shining stars will be a bright galaxy, and it is far better to be the brightest galaxy than a galaxy with just one bright, shining star. I repeated this refrain often because I wanted everyone to know that I wanted each and every employee to succeed and to shine, because I wanted everyone to embrace and nurture an environment that provided for all the opportunity to do so, and because this wasn't the business ethos of the organization when I joined it.

WHILE THE BUSINESS ETHOS WAS something I worked to change during my years with the organization, the structure of the organization was in most regards immutable.

I can best describe that structure by likening it to a bicycle wheel. Al was at the center of the wheel and all employees and departments emanated from that hub, as spokes on a bicycle wheel emanate from its center.

Al often expressed to me that he did not want and that we did not have a chain of command. "We have no chain of command," he often proudly declared. He meant, of course, that we had no chain of command beyond him.

Al did not believe in, and thus most employees did not have, titles. Those who did generally bestowed them upon themselves or upon those with whom they worked closely and those titles were not particularly instructive. They were, like the organizational structure itself, amorphous. For my first decade or so as a full-time employee, I did not have a title, nor did I want one. I don't think titles are necessary or important. Were it not for the fact that a fellow employee pushed Al to permit and to grant more traditional titles, we wouldn't have implemented that practice. So yes, I was given a "big title," but that did not change Al's view or our structure: no chain of command.

I discussed this subject with Al many times over the years and remarked to him that I was surprised by his views, as he so often cited the military as an example of a structure that he admired and that he believed worked, and the military is hierarchical; there is a clear chain of command.

Al acknowledged that was a fair point, but reiterated that a hierarchical or pyramid structure wasn't one he wanted for the Raiders.

I saw merit in the structure that Al preferred and, indeed, mandated. It can be effective and create an exciting work environment if the person at the center of that bicycle wheel is fully engaged with all parts of the organization. But it presented a challenge for us, as Al chose not to engage with all parts of the organization. That was his right as the owner – he should not have to do so if he did not wish to; he could delegate such responsibility to others. But to be effective, such a delegation of responsibility must be accompanied by authority necessary to effectuate those responsibilities. I quickly learned that responsibility without authority is a bad combination. While I labored under that limitation throughout my career, I recognized that I was no more limited in that regard than every Raiders head coach and every Raiders defensive coordinator.

A different structure I believe can be effective and can create an exciting, productive work environment is one I liken to a Venn diagram – one in which all departments are drawn as circles, each overlapping with others to differing degrees. Such a structure recognizes that because each department affects all others, none should operate as autonomous units. It is the antithesis of a silo approach to business.

While I saw merit in the structure Al mandated (assuming that the invidual at the hub of the wheel interacted with all others), and while I love my Venn-diagram approach to business, I knew that not everyone did.

The absence of (indeed, the mandate that we not implement) a truly hierarchical, pyramid structure and the lack of a clear chain of command were disconcerting to many employees, many of whom criticized and complained about it. On countless occasions over the years, I explained to prospective and existing employees that I understood and respected their views, but that if they were not comfortable with or did not like this sort of structure, then our organization might not be the right place for them.

Our organization was the right place, however, if an employee wished to work in an environment that encouraged growth and advancement. The best businesses encourage employees who wish to grow and to advance to do so. I find it stupefying that all businesses don't do that and that some businesses actually affirmatively discourage employees from working to grow and advance. That's nuts. If a business fails to encourage – or actively discourages – its employees from growing and advancing, those employees wishing to grow and advance will leave to do so. That's inverse Darwinism, in the business sense.

I grew and advanced within the organization and I wanted others to have that opportunity as well. As of the time I am writing this, the organization remains full of employees who grew and advanced within it, in some cases from the most entry-level positions to very prominent ones.

I always wanted Al to interact with everyone on staff and I prevailed upon him time and again to do so. He let me know in no uncertain terms that he wasn't interested in doing that and that I should stop pestering him about it (although he didn't express this quite so delicately).

I always tried to include other employees in my interactions with Al, even when it wasn't appropriate to do so, and even though by so doing I annoyed the hell out of him. "*You* can work with other people." he told me. "I don't want to."

I failed to accomplish this for all employees and I failed to do this in each instance in which I wished to do so, but I kept trying. Interestingly, although Al told me not to do it – and although he was angry with me when I did – there were instances in which he seemed to enjoy those interactions with others. Not many, but some. With the exception of only one employee I can think of, I don't believe that the employees I included in those conversations and meetings knew that I was yelled at by Al for including them. It wasn't important to me that they knew how difficult it was to arrange for their inclusion or how angry it made Al, and it would have defeated many of the reasons for which I was including them. Similarly, I never told them of the instances in which Al told me that they should be fired.

I pleaded with Al on many occasions to address the entire staff as a whole, in any setting he wished. I told him that I would arrange anything he wanted, at any time of day or night, so that everyone could see him and hear from him and learn from him and be inspired by him. I wanted him to share his passion for the Raiders with the entire staff – I wanted him to share what it meant to be a Raider. I was never able to convince him to do so.

Another piece of advice I received was from a league executive: "Never hire anyone smarter than you." That was – and remains – one of the dumbest things I have ever heard. I told this person that I hoped to hire only people I believed were smarter than I. Hiring the smartest people makes everyone smarter and makes an organization better. Colleagues should make one another, and thus the organization for which they work, better. My colleagues made me better than I otherwise would have been and I hope that I made them better than they otherwise would have been. That league executive – the one who said he never hires anyone he thinks is smarter than he is – still works in the league office and he's now an even more senior executive.

AS NOTED, FOOTBALL IS A business. Stated more precisely, the NFL and its member clubs are businesses – very big businesses that have grown astronomically over the last two or three decades. Though all of the clubs are in the same business, each approaches this business in a different manner.

Very early in my career – over a decade before Al named me CEO – I was asked to identify what I believed would be a significant challenge for the league in the decades to come. My answer was that I foresaw an ever-increasing revenue differential between and among clubs, and this revenue differential would result in changes in the way the league and clubs did business.

I anticipated that the growing revenue differential would be driven in large part by two factors: (a) a growing difference of opinion as to desired profitability; and (b) beyond that, a necessary shift based upon the escalating cost of franchises. Owners who paid tremendous sums for their franchises and who had significant acquisition debt associated therewith would have a very different view as to the importance of profit (and the amount needed) than did owners who inherited their clubs or paid relatively little for them. In some instances, therefore, profitability was necessary. In other instances, while profitability was not essential, it was desired. Different owners placed a different emphasis on profit.

Whether profit was required or desired, each club prioritized and balanced football operations and business operations differently. I never believed that football and business imperatives and goals need be mutually exclusive, but I did understand that at times, compromise would be required.

Al did not believe that there should be any sort of compromise or balance whatsoever and he made it absolutely clear that football operations were to be our only concern and our entire focus. We were thus precluded from engaging in any and all business practices he believed might adversely impact football operations, even when compelling arguments could be made that they would not. Many people very closely related to or associated with Al endorsed his views.

I remember, on many occasions, listening to people tell Al: "You're right, these things are ridiculous, we didn't used to do these things." *Well, that's right; you didn't*, I thought, *but when you began in football, there were no suites, no club seats, no premium seating products, no naming rights, no integrated media and advertising programs, no cross-platform sponsorships, no large community events, and no Internet for that matter.*

Oh, and there was also not a quarter of a billion or so dollar annual revenue differential between the lowest and the highest revenue club.

The world evolves. If you choose not to adapt your business practices, then don't bemoan not being able to compete economically, as to do so is disingenuous.

Sponsors, suite purchasers, premium product purchasers, radio and local television rights holders, naming rights purchasers, and other business partners want access. They want access to players, the coach, the general manager, and the owner. They want access to all the inner circles and inner workings of the organization. They want the cachet that comes with being a business partner or top spender with the organization.

No matter how much and how often I prevailed upon Al (it really was downright begging, in many instances), he just wouldn't agree that we could engage in these sorts of business practices. Ultimately, my goal was less lofty. I just wanted him to stop kicking our sponsors and suite holders and business partners off the practice field at training camp or from the locker room while on a tour of our facility. Those things happened a lot. We'd be hosting an event that included a tour of our locker room and Al would decide that he wanted to work out – so he would send an employee down to kick out our guests. It would have been nice if those in the league who were critical of our business practices and our revenues understood the magnitude of these challenges.

Al's view was that all we needed to do was win, and that the fans and revenues would simply flow in. Assuming for the moment that his worldview was correct, then one still had to win, consistently.

Al's view on these topics extended to the head coach as well. He did not want nor allow anyone to "bother" the coach. So while we might have been able to entice a potential business partner with access to our coach in lieu of Al (since we couldn't offer access to him), we were never able to include that term in a deal. In some organizations, the owner sends a loud, clear message to the head coach that he must cooperate with those in the organization who are working to engage clients and customers. In our organization, the loud, clear message was just the opposite: leave the coach alone. Again, if this how one chooses to proceed, fine – but then don't complain about not being able to compete economically.

A fun aside: there was one (and only one) occasion during my career on which Al attended a meeting with a prospective or contracted sponsor. Throughout that meeting, Al repeatedly referenced "the swish." I kept whispering to him "swoosh, not swish," but it didn't help. We didn't enter an agreement with that company – as we didn't with many – as Al would not agree to terms necessary to do so.

At one league meeting, Jerry Jones stood before the room and shared his excitement about a creative, impressive marketing deal he generated for what were then huge dollars. Jerry had introduced to the league an innovative approach to marketing and business, and he changed the perception and behavior of many with respect thereto. Al was sitting behind me during Jerry's presentation and he kept jabbing me with his finger, right between two ribs, throughout it. As he did, he repeatedly and loudly asked, in a disgusted and accusatory tone: "What the fuck is wrong with us, why can't we get deals like that?"

Jerry then explained that as part of this new sponsorship relationship with a retailer, his head coach would model the sponsor's products in its national catalogue and he (Jerry) would travel to a number of locations throughout the country and give motivational speeches to the sponsor's employees. I turned to Al, smiled like the cat that ate the canary, and said: "That's why." Al never raised that topic again.

I could never convince Al that it was irrational and disingenuous for him to restrict our ability to raise revenue all the while criticizing staff for failing to do so and complaining that we weren't able to compete economically. We argued about this for decades. As was the case when we argued about revenue sharing, I never believed he had a reasonable response.

One area in which we were ahead of other clubs and the league in terms of fan connectivity and global reach was this: we offered content on our website in many languages, including Tagalog, Chinese, Spanish, and German, and we offered radio broadcasts in Navajo. I was very passionate about these initiatives, and I was surprised that when I first told Al of them, he didn't seem particularly interested. After all, it was he who first and often said, "The Raiders are global." But over time, he periodically asked me about them in a manner that suggested that he liked that we were offering Raiders content in many languages. And, of course, these initiatives didn't require granting the access he precluded.

Al also had interesting views about the profit that television networks should realize from broadcast rights. After one league meeting that Al didn't attend, I shared with him the terms of new network television deals that were discussed and explained that league officials believed that the deals optimized profit for both the teams and networks. Al response as to the networks: "Oh fuck them, why should they make any money?" To paraphrase one of Al's favorite phrases, he missed the point.

THESE CHALLENGES WERE A BYPRODUCT of Al's unique approach to life and business. They made our jobs harder, but all jobs come with challenges and I wouldn't have traded working with Al and for the Raiders for anything.

I did not share with league employees or owners or employees of other clubs that these challenges existed, and with the exception of only one or two senior people with whom I worked closely, I did not discuss them with other Raiders employees. Of course, some employees knew that some of these challenges existed – they saw what went on – but I don't think that they understood the magnitude of the challenges. On many occasions, when someone presented a really terrific, creative proposition, I turned it down because I had failed in my efforts to convince Al to change his mind about such things, and I knew that if we proceeded, he would order us to cancel the project. But I certainly wasn't going to blame Al. I wanted to protect him as best I could, so I simply said no. Employees were thus disappointed and angry with me. Better that, though, than with Al.

It was absolutely Al's right to dictate business practices, as long as he understood and was willing to accept the ramifications.

Ultimately, our differing views on these topics didn't matter, as the league office eventually began dictating club business practices in these and related areas.

One such area was stadium entertainment, a topic about which Al had strong views.

Al staunchly opposed showing or announcing in stadium the scores of other games, particularly those that could affect our standings or impact our playoff chances, and he prohibited us from doing so. He believed it would be detrimental to our team's performance if the players knew the outcome of those games.

That meant that we could not accept revenue for "highlights from around the league" or otherwise provide scoring updates. That also meant that in the day before Internet connectivity in stadiums, fans were in the dark as to what was going on around the league.

Ultimately, of course, technology emerged enabling fans to access any information they wanted on their phones. A funny moment occurred in this regard after this technology was available: in order to make the playoffs, we needed to win the game we were playing, and we also needed

Denver to lose the game it was playing. Well, Denver lost its game while our game was still ongoing. Our fans knew that Denver had lost and they also knew that we wouldn't announce that in the stadium – so our magnificent fans, hoping to inspire the team, began chanting, "Den–ver lost! Den–ver lost!" Technology rendered our policy moot. Then, the league overrode it.

As the league became increasingly aware that more and more needed to be done to attract fans to stadiums, it began both allowing clubs to do in-stadium things that it had previously prohibited and mandating that clubs engage in certain activities. In so doing, it took away from clubs many entertainment and other in-stadium decisions. By way of example, the league adopted a policy mandating that teams show highlights from around the league periodically throughout each game.

I recall one two per club league meeting in which a very senior league executive stated bluntly that owners must end the practice of allowing coaches and others he referred to as *football people* from dictating, or even weighing in on, decisions with respect to in-stadium entertainment. Using stadium music as an example, he stated, "You must take these decisions away from your *football people* and make these decisions yourself." He was didactic and dismissive, noting that owners must no longer allow such people to proffer the argument that certain music or any aspect of the in-stadium experience might prove to be a competitive disadvantage.

It was clear to me that: (a) he used the expression *football people* in a pejorative sense; and (b) he didn't understand that in our case the owner *was* a football person. And Al did have strong views about in-stadium experience and he ruled out certain entertainment because he believed it would hurt our chances of winning. I remember thinking to myself that it would be funny if this executive knew that in our case, nothing would be solved by asking the owner to stop the practice of allowing football people to make these decisions because the owner was a football person and he had issued these dictates.

This instance was not the first time that I sensed that this executive had some disdain for – or perhaps just a lack of interest in – those he called *football people*. It was my impression that this executive did not love the game of football. That said, he is a tremendous businessman – very accomplished and very successful. It is not an overstatement to note that this executive has been the most pivotal league employee in terms of transforming the league into the colossal business it is today.

Over the course of many years, I became troubled by the diminishing number of league office employees who have a tremendous passion for the game itself. I have long believed that the league would be better if there were more football people (and I use that expression in a very complimentary sense) in senior positions in the league office, and I am glad that the current commissioner has added people who played or coached the game or who worked in other capacities at clubs. While the league office is replete with tremendously well-educated, talented, accomplished individuals who hold a variety of positions and with whom I enjoyed working throughout my career, I hope the league continues to add people who love the game.

An interesting interaction with a league employee involved the movie *Draft Day*. I was asked to read the script, and after I did I contacted the woman in the league office who had suggested to the producers that they send it to me. At the outset of that conversation, she enthusiastically volunteered that she was thrilled that the movie included such a "strong female character." I listened for a bit and then shared with her that I was disappointed that a plot device involved this character having a romantic relationship with the general manager, the character to whom she reported. The woman with whom I was speaking seemed genuinely surprised by my observation and responded by explaining that this had never occurred to her, nor had any of the large group of senior league executives who had read the script raised that issue. She told me who those executives were and I was surprised, as I knew those men and had worked with them for years. Do I believe that these men think that female employees (at clubs or in the league office) should have romantic or sexual relationships with their superiors? No. Do I believe that they considered this plot device and concluded that it was a good idea that should be advanced? No. I don't think that they gave that plot device any thought whatsoever or that this occurred to them, and that surprised me. Quite a few women who work in the league office have laughed at me for being surprised.

To this day, I am asked whether that character reminds me of me. The individuals posing that question do so excitedly, in a manner that suggests that they think that's a compliment. I respond by noting that I never had a romantic or sexual relationship with the general manager or with anyone at work. Is that an ungracious response? Yes, I suppose it is. Do I understand that this movie is a work of fiction? Yes. All of that said, I just don't think it was necessary for this character to have the relationship that she did with her boss.

JUST AS ORGANIZATIONS GRAPPLE WITH the issue of balancing certain imperatives and goals with others, they grapple with how to define success. The tension between the quest for immediate success and proceeding in a manner designed to achieve sustained success, and the dilemma as to whether to evaluate success on a short- or long-term basis, are fascinating and fundamental issues for all businesses, but they are, perhaps, more evident and pronounced in sports. Some organizations do a better job at addressing these issues than others.

As a general rule, owners own for a very long time. These businesses are often passed from one generation to the next. Owners have the luxury of focusing on the long term, while for the most part, general managers and coaches do not.

The current collective bargaining agreement has made it more difficult to churn a roster, but owners can churn coaches and general managers and some do so with great frequency.

Even when a general manager or coach enters what is considered a long-term contract in the football sense, those contracts can be terminated at any time with relatively little financial impact on the organization.

A general manager or coach with only a few years on his contract is most often not focused on or worrying about the health of the team years in the future when he likely won't be there; he's focused on and worried about his job security, about winning now. So when a team is struggling and a coach or general manager believes he is on the proverbial hot seat, he may well take action designed to spur immediate, rather than long-term, improvement. Most individuals do what they think necessary to survive.

I believe this is one of the reasons why those individuals making football decisions (whom to draft, what free agents to sign, whether or not to make a trade) rarely act in contravention of conventional wisdom. John Maynard Keynes noted: "Worldly wisdom teaches that it is better for reputation to fail conventionally than to succeed unconventionally." Keynes might well have been referring to NFL general managers and personnel executives when he made that observation – in fact, I have jokingly wondered publicly whether he was.

It takes courage to do the unconventional. It takes courage to draft someone, sign someone, trade for someone, or hire someone when conventional wisdom holds that it is incorrect to do so.

It became apparent to me early in my career that most general managers and personnel executives are scared to do anything that may be perceived as unconventional or different. After all, if one does the conventional, one is far less likely to be criticized, even when one fails when so doing.

I observed that many general managers and personnel executives listen to their peers around the league and to the (often self-proclaimed) experts far too much (while asserting that they do not). Thus, events like the draft often appear to be what I refer to as the march of the lemmings. I don't know if lemmings actually march, but if they do, I'll bet they look a lot like general managers and personnel executives.

Obviously, there are exceptions to this generalization. A few organizations have done a tremendous job in recent years of marching to their own beat – criticism and critics be damned – and have achieved success while so doing.

Al was never concerned with conventional wisdom and he certainly marched to the beat of his own drum. At times he met with tremendous success and at other times he failed, but no matter what one's view of those decisions, it is indisputable that Al was unconcerned with what others thought of him.

10

THE HIGGINS BOAT

FOOTBALL IS FULL OF PLATITUDES AND PRONOUNCEMENTS, AS is business, as is life. I find the vast majority of them annoying:

We have to take it one game at a time.
We just have to play our game.
It's not a sprint, it's a marathon.
He's a guy.
He's just a guy.
We have to play within ourselves.
He plays the game the right way.
He's a character guy.
He's a class guy.
We have to take it to another level.
We're going to do things the right way.
We're going to be built on toughness.
We're going to attack in all three phases of the game.
We just have to do a few things.
We did a few things.
We're going to play for 60 minutes.
We're going to give 100 percent.

There is one pronouncement I heard time and again throughout my career that I find particularly annoying: *No one understands how hard it is.*

I heard this countless times from umpteen coaches and many others in the industry over the course of my career. I heard this each year during training camp and I heard this throughout the season. *No one understands how hard it is* or, alternatively, *You just don't understand how hard this is.*

When I heard this during training camp, I was bemused. Okay, you're standing on a football field, in the warmth of the afternoon sun, in the Napa Valley, telling me that *no one understands how hard it is.* You are staying in a nice hotel, your every need is handled, your clothing is provided to you and then washed for you, your meals are provided, almost anything you request will be delivered to you, and you're telling me that *no one understands how hard it is.* I had similar thoughts when I heard this during the season. Okay, you're earning millions of dollars and you're telling me that *no one understands how hard it is.* A car is provided for you and gassed and washed for you, your clothing is provided to you and then washed for you, your meals are provided to you, your dry cleaning picked up and delivered, almost any convenience will be provided and you're telling me that *no one understands how hard it is.*

This mentality – that it's *so hard* – is prevalent in the NFL. This refrain is repeated over and over – people really believe that everything is "so hard" and that they work harder than anyone else in the whole world. Al said to me on many occasions that "being a head coach in the NFL is the hardest job in the world." Occasionally, he'd add, "Except maybe for being the president of the United States." He said that very sincerely – he really wasn't sure that being president of the United States was as hard as being a head coach, but he was willing to concede that it might be.

I was there; I know how hard coaches worked, and in some cases, did not work. I know about the coaches and others who claimed that they worked almost 24 hours a day and did not.

I'm not suggesting that the job is not hard – it is. I'm not suggesting that coaches don't work hard – they do. I'm not suggesting that the job is not stressful – it is. I'm not suggesting that the public scrutiny and second-guessing isn't hard on coaches and their families – they are. The job is full of pressure and stress and, at times, long hours. Coaches are questioned and second-guessed by ownership, the media, and fans. Coaches and their families are subjected to all kinds of invective.

But coaches and others in the NFL earn a lot of money for their work and for this stress. And while they do work long hours on many days during the season, they do not work long hours every day. They also get a lot of time off after the end of one season and before the start of the next. I'm certainly not aware of many jobs in which people have that amount of time off.

It always struck me that some perspective was (and is) needed. Working in a coal mine is hard and not as lucrative. Working as an air traffic controller at a busy airport is stressful and not as lucrative. Working three jobs at minimum wage to feed a family is hard and stressful and not as lucrative. Serving the country in a hostile environment is beyond compare.

I don't want to minimize the hard work and stress associated with coaching or working in football, but from a cost-benefit perspective, one must recognize the benefits, as well as the costs.

I have discussed this topic with a number of current and former coaches for whom I have tremendous respect and admiration. Some acknowledged that the points I raised were fair; others disagreed. Some offered additional factors for me to consider.

They noted that the anger that fans direct at coaches and their families when things are not going well is unlike anything employees in most other industries experience. They are right. The children of coaches are hassled – often mercilessly – when the team their father coaches is not doing well. Their wives are confronted and subjected to invective when running errands. Coaches really can't go anywhere without receiving input, scrutiny, and often scorn. Even when stopped at a red light, one noted, he was subjected to vitriol.

It is obviously and of course unconscionable for anyone to yell at a child when a team coached by his or her father is doing poorly. There is just no scenario in which that is remotely acceptable – it defies logic and reason that this occurs.

The coaches who shared these thoughts with me are correct. My point is, though, that other jobs are also hard and stressful but don't come with any of the benefits that football provides. With benefits come burdens.

That sort of harassment is not limited to coaches and their families. Anyone who was known to work for the organization was fair game for criticism when getting coffee, running errands, dining out, or attending public events.

Coaches and their families were also not the only ones associated with the team who were subject to vitriol on game day. I recall stopping by to see my then roughly 75-year-old father in his seat at halftime of a game and hearing an angry fan loudly express his displeasure with me by using a word that rhymes with *front*. My dad looked at me and I quickly said: "He said punt, Dad; he was angry that we had to punt before halftime." While others in the organization experienced this sort of thing, coaches certainly experienced it more.

Perspective is important.

No matter how hard we worked, our jobs were exciting and often fun, they came with tremendous benefits, and we were privileged to hold them. Certainly, not every moment was fun and circumstances and situations could be tremendously difficult, challenging, and stressful, but we were fortunate to be doing what we did.

I EMPHASIZED THE CONCEPT OF perspective the night the league announced it was locking out the players in March 2011.

This was a time of tremendous uncertainty in the industry. We didn't know if the season would be truncated or if there would be a season at all. Employees were concerned about job security and compensation. There had been rumblings for months that if there was a lockout, clubs would institute layoffs or pay cuts for the duration of it, and the moment the lockout was announced, some clubs did just that. Employees who had relied on each paycheck to handle financial obligations (rent, food, childcare) feared that we too might institute pay cuts or layoffs.

In the moments immediately after the lockout was announced, I called a staff meeting for all employees of the organization and explained four things.

One: I didn't know how long the lockout would last or what would transpire, but I would share everything I knew and learned as I learned it. My door would be, as always, open, and everyone was, as always, encouraged to ask me anything they wished.

Two: We would approach and surmount this challenge together.

Three: In lieu of layoffs or salary reductions designed to address the challenges presented by the lockout, we would instead institute a plan that I believed was exciting and would be fun. This plan, I explained, was designed to be productive rather than confiscatory and would apply to every employee in the organization – the head coach, me, every employee – we would do this together. Each of us would be required to sell an amount of seating product equal to ten percent of our salary for each month of the lockout. Employees would not, however, be required to complete those sales until the start of the season. This program (the ten percent threshold, the date by which sales were required) was designed with this goal in mind: that everyone succeed. I also wanted everyone to have fun. I explained that employees could collaborate with one another and pool their talents and strengths. Of course, if they preferred, they could work individually. No matter whether they chose to work alone or in groups, I emphasized that our entire ticket team would be delighted to help everyone achieve their goals.

To the annoyance of many of the club's longest-tenured employees, I had for decades advanced the notion that we were all representatives of the organization, and thus had a responsibility to engage in community activities as Raiders, to promote the organization, and to help fill the stadium, sell our products, and to further all of our goals.

In this instance, even those employees who had for decades objected to those views and refused to do those things embraced this opportunity to promote and market the organization and the plan was well received.

Some employees shared with me that they were ecstatic. Many had been extremely worried about what would happen to them in a lockout and feared that we might do what other clubs were doing. Some employees shared with me that they were relieved, but that they had trepidation as they had never tried to sell and were nervous about the prospect of so doing. I reminded them that our goal was, and the plan was designed, to best enable everyone to succeed.

It should always be the goal of every business that every employee succeed and businesses should best position employees to do so, just as coaches should best position players to succeed.

I was thrilled with our plan to address the challenges presented by the lockout and I was proud of the way our employees responded to it.

Many employees of other clubs told me that they wished that their employer had implemented a plan like ours. Owners of several other clubs told me that they loved the plan and wished their clubs had also implemented a creative approach to the challenges which might be presented by a lockout.

I also heard from executives of clubs which had instituted what I referred to as confiscatory plans who told me quite pointedly that they didn't appreciate my using the word *confiscatory* to describe plans such as the ones they put in effect.

Four: Perspective is important. To illustrate this point, I shared a story about Lloyd Blankfein, the CEO of Goldman Sachs. As he and a Goldman employee were emerging from cars to head into the New York Federal Reserve for one of many meetings about the 2008 financial crisis, the employee groaned to Blankfein that he didn't think that he could take another day of hearings. Blankfein responded, "You're getting out of a Mercedes to go to the New York Federal Reserve; you're not getting out of a Higgins boat on Omaha Beach."

Those words are among the wisest I have ever heard uttered in a business – no, in any – context. In an absolutely spectacular, sensational manner, Blankfein reminded or taught this employee to keep things in perspective.

Exactly. Perspective. You're working for a football team involved in a labor dispute; you're not getting out of a Higgins boat on Omaha Beach.

When I shared the story, I told everyone assembled that if they didn't know what a Higgins boat was, they should Google it. Perhaps I should have said "oogle," as Al did to me.

One employee shared with me a few days later that when she got home that night, she told her husband about the staff meeting and the Blankfein story I had shared as her young son listened. The next morning, as she expressed some trepidation, her son said, "Mommy, don't worry; you told us you're not getting out of a Higgis [sic] boat."

I sent a note to Lloyd explaining that his words were among the most profound and powerful I had ever heard, that I had shared them with the entire Raiders staff, and that they were being shared across multiple generations.

When we learned that the lockout was over and that the season would not be truncated, I again gathered everyone together and explained that since no games would be missed, our program would be modified. Now, no one would be required to make any sales and those who had already done so would be paid the standard commission in place at all times for our commissioned sales staff. I thought that was fair – those employees who had already started to fulfill (or in some cases, completely fulfilled) their sales requirement should be rewarded. It would not have been right to treat those who had already performed – in whole or in part – the same as those who had not yet performed. I was touched when some employees told me that they appreciated our approach to the lockout and that they planned to perform even though they were no longer required to do so and I was touched when some employees requested that I direct commissions they had already earned to our tickets for kids and tickets for troops programs instead.

BACK TO PLATITUDES AND PRONOUNCEMENTS.

Although I don't like platitudes and often make fun of them, I acknowledge that on occasion I used them, too. When standing on the practice field at training camp, fielding questions from people with whom I was guarded – people with whom I didn't have a relationship of trust – it was easier to speak in platitudes, and I did.

"He's a guy," I might say about a particular player.

"That's why we play the games," might be my response if asked whether we would beat a particular team.

Platitudes aside, I loved training camp. While the team was in Los Angeles, training camp was a bit up the coast in Oxnard and when the team moved back to Oakland, it was in the Napa Valley. Whether I attended to entertain business partners, to meet with Al or other owners, to entertain community groups, or to meet with others in the organization or league executives, we stood outside and watched practice.

We stood immediately on the sideline when watching practice and sometimes, play would come quickly toward us. On one of my first visits to camp, I committed to myself that I would never flinch when the action came toward me. I also decided on one of those early visits that it was not a good idea to run on the field to break up a fight.

As to my no-flinch policy, after a play once came directly toward me at a very high rate of speed and I didn't budge, Tim Brown took a moment to walk toward me and to say, while shaking his head, "Amy, back up so you don't get killed." I still never flinched.

We drafted Tim in the first draft after I joined the organization on a full-time basis. At one point, I told Al that Tim and I were in the same draft class, to which he dryly responded: "Tim was a first-round pick; you were a street free agent." He was right on both counts.

There are occasional fights at every training camp throughout the league. On one of my first visits to camp, a fight broke out fairly close to me. I immediately thought of the prospect of injury to our players and my instinctive reaction was to run on to the field to try to separate them. As I started toward the fight, someone grabbed me from behind and stopped me dead in my tracks. As I struggled to run toward the fight, he held firmly, laughing as he said, "Whoa girl, don't do that." It was Willie Brown, who looked after me throughout my career. He was right. They had helmets – I did not.

Another defensive back once had some fun at camp at my expense. As I stood on the sideline with our guests watching defensive-back drills, I decided to explain some techniques and coverage schemes. As I spoke, I noticed that they were looking at me intently, wide eyed. *Boy, I must be doing a good job*, I thought. *They're captivated.* So, emboldened, I continued on at some length. Only after a few more moments went by did I sense a presence behind me and turn to find George Atkinson. George had a large grin on his face and was pretending to take notes as I offered these insights.

Although I loved camp, there were challenges. I hated having to dance around the issue of why Al would not spend time with our sponsors, broadcast partners, business partners, and others. I don't know of another club owner who does not spend time with these constituents. Al did not do so, whether at camp or otherwise.

But that aside, I loved training camp.

11
THAT BABY'S GOING TO CANTON

WORKING FOR THE RAIDERS WAS A PRIVILEGE I NEVER TOOK FOR granted – not for one day. Even when I was exasperated or angry or both, I considered it a privilege.

I didn't love everything about my job, but I loved my job. I hated certain things about my job, but I loved my job. I disagreed with Al; I argued with Al; I wanted to change things that I was not allowed to change, but I loved my job.

There were times that I was particularly exasperated and angry. One of those was what is known as the overhead projector press conference.

On a number of occasions over the years, I told Al that I disagreed with his propensity to make coaching changes. In this instance, I also vehemently disagreed with him about the manner in which he was handling a prospective coaching change, and we had been arguing about this for months.

I was furious in large part because of the deleterious effect this was having on the organization and Al was furious with me because I did not support his position and because I continuously expressed my anger to him. We were at one another's throats. I actually quit my job over this.

Al and Lane Kiffin had been angry with each other for some time. They disagreed with one another on a number of football matters – particularly with respect to player personnel and assistant coaches. Of course, Lane wasn't the only Raiders head coach who disagreed with Al about such matters, but he was less surreptitious in the manner in which he expressed his disagreement. As their disagreements escalated in number and intensity, Al engaged in behavior that struck me as his way of saying "fuck you" to Lane. What differentiated Lane from most men with whom Al interacted over many years was that Lane engaged in behavior that I considered his way of saying, "No, fuck *you*." Despite the fact that all of this was playing out publicly and harming the organization, I begrudgingly respected that Lane was not cowed by Al.

I wanted them to work together and I urged Al repeatedly to try to find a way to do so. Those conversations didn't go well. I pointed out to Al that he and Lane shared a number of traits in common. Unfortunately, it seemed those commonalities did not strengthen their relationship, but worsened it. It was like trying to push together the same polar end of two magnets – the magnets don't attract one another; they repel one another.

I didn't attend the overhead projector press conference. I was mad at Al and I did not want to be there. Al was mad at me and I had the sense that he did not want me there. Neither of us was acting particularly maturely. Should I have nonetheless attended so that we appeared to be united and so that I could help if possible? I probably should have. As it turned out, other than racing to the outlet into which the projector was plugged and ripping the cord from it or finding the power source to the building or the fuse box and killing power in the auditorium, I could not have helped. Had I been there, I think I would have considered going to any lengths to disable that overhead projector, even if to do so I had to bite through its cord with my teeth. In any event, I didn't attend. I stayed in my office. Two of my coworkers joined me and we turned on the television to watch.

The minute the press conference began, I noticed that Al wasn't sitting in front of our logoed backdrop, which always hung behind the speaker or speakers during press conferences, and I said, "Hey, where's the backdrop? Why isn't the sponsor backdrop up? Why does it look whited-out?" We looked at one another, but none of us knew. When we realized that a white screen had been set up behind Al, obscuring the backdrop, we looked quizzically at one another, as we didn't know why that was the case. I will never forget the look on the face of one of my coworkers as the cameras pulled back and we saw the overhead projector. I imagine the look on my face was the same. I didn't even know we had an overhead projector.

We soon understood why the overhead projector was there: Al had instructed someone to project on the screen a copy of a letter he and another employee had drafted and which they had sent to Lane. Al then led the assembled media through a thorough, line-by-line analysis of the letter, which detailed what Al believed to be each and every one of Lane's transgressions.

I remember saying to my coworkers with whom I was watching the press conference: "If we're going to do something this insane, can't we at least use modern technology?" I understood, of course, that the technology we employed was the least of our problems.

As we watched the press conference, I was speechless. The three of us were speechless. We sat there in silence, looking at one another. I am sure that the look on my face was the same as the look I saw on their faces – a mixture of horror and anger and despair. I knew that our phones would already be ringing off the hook – fans, ticket holders, sponsors, suite holders, and business partners would already be calling. And they were. I knew that it would take extraordinary effort to do any sort of damage control and that, really, even extraordinary efforts might not work.

I gathered myself as best I could. I knew that I needed – and I wanted – to be a calming presence with our employees and others. But I wasn't calm; I was infuriated and I was disheartened.

I went down and spoke to the women who handled our front desk and our main phone lines. I will never forget the looks on their faces. The phones were, indeed, already ringing incessantly. I then went and spoke with our customer service department, our sponsorship and marketing departments, our ticket personnel, and every other employee I could find. I will never forget the look on the face of a senior ticket executive. He was ashen, and his expression said all that I was thinking and all that I understood others were thinking.

We lost ticket holders, we lost club seat holders, we lost suite holders, we lost sponsors, and we lost business partners. One of my greatest frustrations over the course of my career was that I believed Al was intellectually dishonest about things of this nature. He chose to act without regard to consequences that were both predictable and predicted, but then complained about those consequences. Even when I explained in advance precisely what consequences would flow from his actions, he denied that they would and then complained that they did. Of course things like this would impact revenues. Al didn't believe they should or they would, but of course they did and when that happened, he was angry that revenues were down. You can't have it both ways, I would tell him – you can't act as you wish, without concern or regard for the consequences of your actions, and yet be annoyed by those very consequences. We argued about this for decades.

A few nights after the infamous overhead projector press conference, after several wretched days during which I did my best to calm and reassure everyone, during which we all worked together to calm and reassure ticket holders and fans and suite holders and sponsors and business partners, I went home and had a bit of a meltdown. Just as we were about to go to sleep, I announced to my husband: "I am going to find that overhead projector. I am going to find where it's stored. I am going to pull it out and I am going to smash it with an axe. I am going to smash it into itty bitty pieces and there will never be another overhead projector conference again."

When I was done, my husband said: "Oh no, that baby's going to Canton."

I actually laughed.

AS I MENTIONED, NO MATTER the challenges, no matter the arguments, no matter the stress, I never wavered in my belief that it was a tremendous privilege to work for the organization and for Al, and I regularly expressed this view.

As the years went on, I sensed that fewer and fewer employees believed that working for the Raiders was the privilege or the dream come true it was for me, and that fewer and fewer employees cared as deeply about the organization as did I. Of course, there were some other employees who felt privileged to work for and who cared deeply about the Raiders; I was not alone in that belief, but we sensed that we were a dwindling breed.

I discussed this topic from time to time with one of my coworkers. We agreed that when we took our jobs, we did not do so because we viewed them as good jobs, or because they offered good benefits, or because they provided a path to future opportunities; we did so because we wanted to be Raiders. We also agreed that we were in what was becoming an ever-shrinking minority.

I don't believe that what I have described is unique to the Raiders; I believe it is a phenomenon affecting many businesses. I also believe it is at least somewhat generational. I observed a metamorphosis over my career – applicants and new employees viewed jobs as just that: jobs.

I was often told by my coworkers that my inability to shut off (both literally and figuratively) when I left the office was a tremendous failing on my part. I was told that I needed to leave work at the office. I was told that I needed to learn not to make myself available to Al every moment of every day and every night. I never did shut off, I never did leave work at the office, and I never did make myself unavailable to Al. I never tried, I didn't want to, and I don't believe that to be a failing. I never considered my job to be a job.

Al and I agreed about that: it wasn't a job. Early in my career, while in his office, I noticed that he was looking at me as if he was studying me. The expression on his face was both curious and warm and when I asked him why he was staring at me, he told me that he recognized that he and

I shared something in common that he had not seen in many others: I didn't consider my job to be a job but, rather, a way of life. He was right.

I joined the organization not knowing or contemplating what my future with it might be. I only knew that I was deliriously happy to be a part of it. I didn't care what my role was or my responsibilities were. I simply wanted to contribute. There is nothing I could have been asked to do that I would have considered too menial or unimportant. I could have been told that my responsibilities included picking up used paper cups on the sideline or counting the rolls of ankle tape, and I would have done so to the best of my ability and felt fortunate and proud to do so.

Just as over the course of my career, I observed that job candidates and new employees were increasingly focused on what might be their next position rather than the one for which they were interviewing or had been hired, I noticed another evolution: an entitlement mentality.

This also wasn't unique to the Raiders; it too was a societal trend. I was elated when I read an article in which a writer described and discussed the issue of entitlement. In this story, he recounted a story of a preschool where the words to the children's song "Frere Jacques" had been changed to: "I am special, I am special, look at me, look at me…I am very special, I am very special, look at me." *Well that explains a lot*, I thought.

THERE ARE MANY MISCONCEPTIONS ABOUT Al, the biggest of which is that he did not tolerate disagreement from employees. If that were the case, I would have been fired roughly two weeks after I joined the Raiders as a full-time employee. It was then that we had our first argument. It was big, loud, and profanity-packed.

I was sharing an office with another employee and after practice Al entered the room. He was furious. After listening to him berate the other employee for roughly ten minutes, I realized something: he was wrong.

So, two weeks into my job, I interrupted Al and said: "Excuse me, you're wrong."

Al was standing a few feet from my desk, behind which I was sitting. When I uttered those words, he stopped speaking, and slowly turned towards me. He looked at me in a manner that's difficult to describe. It was a mixture of utter dismay, incredulity, surprise, and anger.

As he stood there looking at me, I again said in a respectful, matter-of-fact tone of voice, "You're wrong." Before I could offer my reasoning for that conclusion or say anything else, he spoke, and he did so in a raised voice. So I raised my voice. He shouted. I shouted back. He yelled. I yelled back. On it went. We yelled, shouted, and hollered at one another. He swore. I did not. I was only about two weeks into my job, after all; I wasn't yet swearing at him.

Finally, after quite a bit of this back-and-forth, in a quiet, calm, relaxed tone, he said: "Okay, I got it, I got it, I understand." The argument was over.

I didn't realize it at the time, but our voices had carried throughout the entire second floor of the building. I later learned that many employees had heard us arguing, that a few had emerged from their offices to find out what was going on, and that some thought that I would be fired. One coworker even brought me boxes and offered to help me pack my things.

I didn't plan to tell Al that he was wrong. It wasn't premeditated or in any way calculated. I didn't tell him that I thought he was wrong in order to assert myself or to establish a paradigm for our working relationship. I gave no thought to the fact that I was about to tell Al Davis that he was wrong. I was just being myself. I thought he was wrong. I told him so. We argued. He agreed with me. It was over.

This interaction may well have set the tone for an almost-three-decade working relationship in which I never hesitated to disagree with Al and in which he knew that I would not hesitate to do so. Over the course of my career, I disagreed with him far more than I agreed with him, and I always let him know when I did. Most of our disagreements were loud and fierce. We swore, we yelled, we argued, we hung up on one another, and we often acted obnoxiously. We sometimes behaved like children. On a few occasions, we went days without speaking to one another – notable because we routinely spoke daily.

I knew from that first argument that if I was going to disagree with Al, I would arm myself with facts. If I disagreed, I would let him know why I disagreed and offer support for my argument. I believed that if I did, he would engage in a discussion, a debate, or an argument, but that if I did not, he would not do so. He certainly did in that first instance. But just because I disagreed with him didn't mean I could convince him I was right. That was rare.

AL KNEW THAT IF HE wanted someone to agree with him without question, I wasn't that person. That bothered him and wore on him at times. *I* bothered him and wore on him at times.

Al and I reached extraordinary levels of frustration with one another. We had ferocious arguments. I think that demonstrated to Al that I would not capitulate because it was the path of least resistance. Al shared with me that there were times when he appreciated that.

He seemed pleased and proud as he told me that another owner said to him after I presented our position in an owners' meeting, "Boy, she isn't scared."

He seemed pleased and proud when he said to me, "You're tough." Other times, he said that in resignation, often after he had failed to convince me to agree with him.

He seemed pleased and proud when he said of me to others while I was in his presence," She doesn't back down." He was right: I wasn't scared and I didn't back down. That certainly didn't work to my benefit within some circles. But my job wasn't to advance my own interests or to promote myself at the expense of the club.

As much as Al may have for the most part liked that I didn't get scared or back down and that I was tough, I know that this frustrated and angered him at times.

AL OFTEN TOLD ME THAT I was a "P.I.T.A." He never pronounced the word (like the bread) – he spelled it out each time: P.I.T.A. "You're a real P.I.T.A." The first time he called me a P.I.T.A. he explained to me that the initials stood for "pain in the ass."

"Yes," I told him, "I'm well aware of what the initials stand for." He was right, I can be a P.I.T.A.

PERIODICALLY, AL TOLD ME THAT he wanted to kill me. I knew he was joking.

He once said: "The next time you do that, I'll fuckin' kill you." (I'm not the only employee to whom he said that, by the way. I recall one incident in particular, involving a free agent we lost, in which he told another employee that he'd "fuckin' kill" him if he ever did that again.) A few times over the years I told Al that I wasn't worried – noting that he could fire me, but he couldn't kill me. He once dryly responded: "You seem rather sure of that."

While Al would not have killed me, it would have been very easy for him to fire me. At no time while employed by the organization did I ever have a contract. For the entirety of my career with the Raiders, I was an at-will employee, which means, in essence, that the organization could terminate me with no outstanding contractual obligations on its part. When Al and I were bickering, I would remind him that I was an at-will employee, to which he would respond, "Yes, you are," to which I would respond, "At will goes both ways."

An interesting point about me never having a contract is that while the league requires clubs to submit for its approval contracts for certain employees – head coaches, general managers, and the ultimate decision maker in the business area (president, CEO) – it never required us to submit one for me. I wondered over the years whether the league would ever instruct us to do so, but it never did. I can think of three reasons that might be the case: (a) it never realized that we hadn't filed one; (b) it knew that even if it demanded that we file one, we would not comply; or (c) it understood that my title notwithstanding, I was not the ultimate decision maker, Al was. I am confident that it was (c), perhaps with a dose of (b) mixed in.

DURING MY FIRST YEAR WITH the organization, I made an affirmative decision that for as long as I had my job, I would do it as I believed best without giving consideration to whether I might be fired and with the knowledge that I could and would walk away at any time I wished. I told my husband that at some point, when Al said to me "fuck you," I would reply, "No, fuck *you*." At that point, I explained, one of two things would happen: either I would be fired, or I would quit. It was important to me that my husband understood that. Not only did he understand, he was in absolute agreement with this approach and we agreed to structure our lifestyle as best we could so that I had the freedom to conduct myself as I wished, fully aware that so doing might result in my termination or my resignation. So, we created a bank account which we named the "fuck you fund." We took a bit of money from each paycheck and deposited it in that account. Doing this gave me the freedom to conduct myself as I believed best, without regard to consequences. I understand that not everyone has the luxury to structure one's lifestyle such that he or she can act as he or she believes best, without concern about job security and so that he or she can walk away as desired, but it sure is optimal. Our decision and ability to do so gave me the freedom to do just that. We maintained that account throughout my entire career with the Raiders and I always did as I believed best without regard to economic consequences. Now, we maintain it for sentimental reasons.

AS NOTED EARLIER, NO ONE could control Al. It was also almost impossible to change his mind. As a general rule, Al was always absolutely confident that he was right. When someone didn't agree with him on a business or legal issue, Al would say, "I'll get him in a room." Al was sure that if he "got him in a room" he could convince that person that he was right. "Okay," I would respond sarcastically and somewhat rudely, "you get him in a room; I'm sure that will solve everything."

I found it fascinating that Al was absolutely convinced that he could get anyone in a room and change that person's mind when it was almost impossible for anyone to change Al's mind.

Actually, few people were willing to try to change Al's mind. I witnessed time and again people boldly state their disagreement with him from the privacy of their own offices, but fail or refuse to express their disagreement to him face-to-face. One of my coworkers coined an expression I believe best describes this behavior – it was rude, but perfectly fitting: "little mouse balls." We used that rude expression from time to time.

I always wondered whether it was a deliberate choice on Al's part to surround himself with people who agreed with him or whether the people he surrounded himself with learned not to disagree with him (at least in front of him) because it was easier and it served them well. I think it was more of the latter.

Given Al's knowledge of and interest in history, I raised the issue of Watergate with him on a few occasions to make this point: surrounding himself with men who did not disagree with him didn't work out so well for Richard Nixon.

While there were definitely occasions on which Al would actively look for people to support his position or to undertake a project for him and while there were plenty around him who were more than willing to do so without question or objection, it is unfair to say that Al refused to work with people who disagreed with him or who told him when they thought he was wrong. After all, I did that for the first time just two weeks into my job and continued to do so for almost three decades.

SOME PEOPLE HAVE REMARKED THAT Al held grudges. I don't know that I would articulate it in that precise manner; I might say instead that Al harbored resentment and held tightly to his anger. No matter the word or phrase one chooses to describe it, Al was steadfast in his positions and he rarely moved from them. As noted earlier, when Al believed he was right, it was hard to convince him he wasn't. When Al believed someone else was wrong, it was hard to convince him to evaluate the situation from a different perspective or to simply let things go.

I am often asked about what caused the rift between Al and Marcus Allen and why it was so deep and longstanding. I really don't know. That surprises people and some don't believe me, but it's true. Obviously, I know that there was a deep divide between these men, but I never understood all of the underlying issues that caused it or nuances with respect thereto, and I don't know why it was so lasting.

The argument that set this in motion occurred early in my career on what I believe was a Saturday morning. I was in my office and I heard very loud voices – shouting – coming from Al's office, which was located directly across the hall from mine. I didn't know at that time who was in Al's office (I later learned that it was Marcus). I didn't know what they were discussing, but it sounded like they were having a very heated exchange. I didn't think too much about the raised voices – after all, people have disagreements, they argue, they shout.

In the days and weeks that followed, it became clear that this disagreement – whatever its genesis – was significant.

I suggested to Al many times over the years that he let it go and move forward. Marcus was, I reminded him, a true Raider legend. No history of the Raiders would be complete without reference to Marcus, I told Al. Sometimes, I would simply say: 17 Bob Trey O. That was the play call when Marcus reversed direction and ran 74 yards for a touchdown in Super Bowl XVIII. It remains one of the greatest plays in Raiders and in Super Bowl history.

In my attempts to resolve this and to convince Al to bridge the divide, I referenced world history and current world events, thinking that Al's affinity for such things might help me persuade him.

I sure got "motherfucked" when I raised this issue, but I never stopped trying. I also never succeeded.

I am also often asked about what transpired between Al and Jon Gruden such that Al decided to trade him. I certainly know more about that situation than I do about what occurred between Al and Marcus, but I don't know everything.

Al had been growing increasingly annoyed with Jon. That certainly wasn't a secret and it wasn't unusual; Al grew annoyed with coaches. I don't know whether Al's increasing disenchantment with Jon was the result of an isolated event or disagreement, whether it was due to an accumulation of events, or whether their relationship had simply run its course. Al's relationships with coaches often ran their course and deteriorated. It was clear in the building that Jon was also growing increasingly annoyed with Al. I don't know whether Jon's increasing frustration with Al was the result of a particular issue or argument, or whether he was simply weary of the way Al did business. I think, though, that it was more the latter.

Although I had recommended that we hire Bill Belichick and Al opted to hire Jon instead, I absolutely understood that Jon was also a good choice and would be good for the organization. I thought that we should do whatever we could to retain him and that failing to do so would be a mistake. I tried to convince Al to find a way to work through whatever issues existed between them. I failed.

I was involved in only two meetings at which Jon's future with the team was discussed. In each of those two meetings with Al and two of my coworkers, and in a number of private conversations with Al, I explained the reasons I thought it important that we keep Jon and I prevailed upon him to do so. I told him that no matter the issues that existed, he needed to find a way to work things out. My coworkers in those meetings did not join me in urging Al to do this. One of those coworkers said only that Al should do what he believed right. The other coworker, who worked very closely with Jon, said nothing.

Throughout this, the coworker who worked closely with Jon was attempting to negotiate a new contract (or an extension of the existing one) with Jon's agent in hopes of retaining him. That employee asked yet another coworker to handle the drafting of such contract. It struck me that the whole manner in which this was being handled was convoluted and goofy, even for us.

I learned of the trade after it occurred. It was one night in February 2002. I don't remember the exact time. My husband and I had been out and as we were walking in from the garage, I heard the phone ringing and I rushed to answer it. "Amy, this is Al," he began, as he always did. I was juggling things in my arms; I was distracted. I heard him reference Jon and I heard the word *trade*. I interrupted and said, "I really don't think this is a good idea; I really don't think we should do this." Al responded by saying "You didn't hear me; I just told you I did it."

OTHER AREAS IN WHICH I failed to convince Al that his approach – and thus the organization's approach – was wrong involved media and public relations.

I tried for years to convince Al that we should be more professional and courteous in our dealings with the media. I explained that comporting ourselves professionally and courteously did not mean we had to share information that he did not want to share. It simply meant that we should, at a minimum, be professional and, hopefully, even polite when declining to comment. Certainly, we didn't need to be rude, abrasive, and obnoxious. The media had a job to do, I explained, noting that while that job often conflicted with his desire to maintain confidentiality, we needed to find a better method of expressing ourselves. I failed.

Throughout my years with the organization – on more occasions than I can recount – Al would say to me, "You're runnin' it" or "Aw fuck, you're runnin' it." Only, I really wasn't "runnin it," if "it" meant the organization. Oh sure, I might have been overseeing many of our business relationships, our banking relationships, our relationship with the league office, and some other relationships and matters, I might have been "runnin'" certain aspects of the business, but I wasn't "runnin'" the organization, as Al suggested.

So, although I was dismayed and mortified by our approach to media and public relations, I was unable to make many discernible changes. I was horrified by some of the things we did, many of which I learned of in ways many people find surprising.

On one occasion, Al decided that he wanted the organization to call a prominent, well-respected member of the media a rumor monger. Al didn't share with me that he planned to do this, just as he often didn't share with me things he believed that I'd object to and thus argue with him about. Instead, he took a path of lesser or no resistance. In this instance, he contacted someone on our public relations staff, and together they crafted a statement calling this journalist a "rumormongerer." So, to be clear: he wanted to call someone a rumor monger and we couldn't even do that right – we used a word that really wasn't a word.

I learned of this when I saw it online. I was horrified and I was furious. I printed out what I had seen and stormed into Al's office with a copy of the comment in my hand, which was shaking, I was so angry. The first thing that I sputtered was: "Mongerer isn't even a word."

Then I just exploded: "You guys came up with this deranged statement…and no one even used spell check…what is this, third grade?… we issue a ranting statement…and we don't even use real words, we invent one…the least we could have done was to use spell check."

"Mongerer isn't even a word!" I shouted again and then stomped out. Yes, stomped.

On another occasion, while I was out of the office at a meeting, there had been quite a scene in our media workroom. I didn't learn about this until I arrived home much later that evening and saw it all over the Internet – it looked like a scene right out of a movie. The video showed a Raiders employee shouting at and gesticulating toward a member of the media – pointing at him and accusing him of things – and then accusing another member of the media of something else. I watched the video and was speechless. I had no idea what to do in the aftermath of this incident. I just knew that I had to do what I could to ease the coming backlash. I contacted the employee who instigated the confrontation. I thought he'd be upset and would want to work together to try to resolve the issue, but he actually seemed to be proud of the manner in which he handled this and he made a point of telling me that Al thought he handled it well. It's possible my impression was wrong – that he was being defensive or that he was trying to calm me down – but it certainly struck me that he believed that he had acted appropriately.

On a number of occasions over the course of my career, I shared with a coworker that I sometimes felt like the good fairy in *Sleeping Beauty*. She was the fairy who hid behind the curtain and who, after the bad fairy had cast her evil spell on Sleeping Beauty (about the prick on the spinning wheel), emerged and cast her own spell, to minimize as best she could the repercussions of the bad spell. The good fairy could not undo the spell cast by the bad fairy; she could only try to do something to mitigate the effects of it.

My coworker's response: "Yup."

As bad as I believed those instances were, they weren't even atop the list of terrible things said of the media internally by many who worked closely with Al. In some instances, when Al was launching a diatribe about a particular member of the media or the media as a whole, these employees would concur and offer their own invective. In other instances, they initiated such commentary. What fascinated and bothered me is that the employee who offered the most invective internally was the most gracious when he interacted with the media, and the most well liked by them.

Another public relations issue about which I nagged Al involved the use of modern technology and social media. "News moves fast," I regularly told him. "It won't help to issue a statement two or three days from now – the story will be dead by then. We need to act quickly." I failed. We'd get killed for something and it would be all over the place – print, radio, television, the Internet — and we'd say nothing. Three days later, Al would want to issue a statement, but by then no one cared.

I also wanted us to break our own news – not always, but sometimes. I wanted to periodically share information on our own properties first (our website, our Twitter account, our Facebook page).

I presented to Al what I believed was a persuasive case that it was intellectually dishonest for him to refuse to allow us to be first with at least some information, or to maintain at least some information for proprietary use, all the while complaining that our dominance in these areas (page hits and followers) was not strong as it should be. If we wished to be prominent and dominant in this space, if we wished to maximize revenues (from our website, for example), then he had to stop prohibiting us from doing things designed to increase revenues.

I also told him that I couldn't fathom why he prohibited us from breaking news, thereby allowing people for whom he had such contempt to do so. When mentioning this to him over and over again, I even resorted to using the word he loved – *ludicrous* – to explain the absurdity of hindering our growth while fostering the growth of those for whom he had such disdain. They were able to attract more viewers, more readers, more followers, and more visitors to their sites by breaking news about us, I explained. "This makes no sense," I would groan. And it didn't.

"You can't stand this guy," I would remind him repeatedly of any number of members of the media, "but you allow him to earn more respect and more credibility when he breaks news about us – he is first, he is accurate – and you're facilitating this."

Trying to explain Twitter and social media to Al was a challenge, but it could be fun. (Not as much fun as trying to explain to him who Beavis and Butt-head were and why they were referenced in a league memo, however.)

Once – and only once – did Al make a point of acquiescing to my requests to share something newsworthy on one of our own platforms. We had been arguing about something entirely unrelated to this topic and in an effort to both mollify and apologize to me, he announced to everyone gathered in his office: "Don't let anyone know about this yet – Amy will want to twit this." And so, that once, we were able to "twit" something before anyone else did.

Al adjusted many words. Tweet became *twit* and Google became *oogle*. On a number of occasions, when Al and I were discussing something, I would say, "I'll Google that." He'd respond by saying, "I don't know what the fuck you're talking about." Soon, though, he knew well enough, and he'd periodically say to me: "Oogle that, will you?" I giggled each time.

I giggled a lot at things Al said. The first time I did so, he looked at me and said, "Are you laughing at me?" I admitted that I was. He really and truly seemed surprised that I was laughing at him. I think he was also surprised that I admitted I was.

I was never able to teach Al to use the word *tweet* instead of twit or *Google* instead of oogle.

ALL OF MY DESIRES TO improve the manner in which the organization dealt with the media aside, I know that I did a really poor job of interacting with the media throughout my career.

I was never able to relax when I spoke with the media as a group and, really, I wasn't able to relax even when I spoke with most members of the media on an individual basis. Of course, there were a few exceptions to that, but for the most part, I was never at ease working with the media. I believe that there were a few reasons for that.

I knew that Al did not want me to speak with the media and that certainly added to my stress and discomfort when I did.

Also, as a general rule, I am a precise and measured speaker, careful and deliberate in my selection of words. I don't do this for legal reasons as some surmised, or really for any particular reason. It's just the way I speak. My precise manner of speaking is noticeable, and it was often brought to my attention by some members of the media, and that added to my discomfort.

I was also very cognizant that when speaking with the media or speaking publicly, I wasn't simply representing myself – I was representing Al and the Raiders organization and my words reflected on the league as a whole. Were I only representing myself, it would have been easier, and I might have learned to relax. It took me a considerable period of time after I began working on television to realize that when I now share my views, I represent only myself. Once I realized that, I began to relax. I'm just now learning that it can actually be fun.

I am also not good at witty banter. Oh, sure, I may eventually think of a witty rejoinder to something, but when I do, it's typically many hours or days after the fact. I also don't like sarcasm, particularly when it is used in an effort to disguise or soften mean remarks. I find sarcasm in a business setting particularly discomfiting. So I was ill at ease even in what were intended to be and should have been relaxed, casual interactions with the media.

I understood that members of the media didn't engage in lighthearted or sarcastic banter with me to make me uncomfortable. I understood that they were simply interacting with me in the same manner in which they interacted with one another. I understood that they may even have been doing so in an effort to be friendly. It wasn't their fault that I was uncomfortable; I was uncomfortable because I am socially awkward in such instances.

I also offended some members of the media. I didn't mean to do so and I wasn't aware at the time that I had had done so, but I later learned that I did. An incident that stands out occurred at a game in Kansas City. It was just before kickoff of our game, and the televisions in the press box were showing the early games. One of those was the 49ers game, which was reaching an exciting conclusion. Some of the media were watching and commenting aloud, as the anthem preceding our game began. Without thinking, I shushed one of those members of the media. I did it instinctively – the anthem had begun and I said, "Shhh." I didn't do so with the intent to be rude – and I didn't think I did so loudly – but I said "shhh" – and I thought nothing of it.

Over a decade later, I was told by a several other members of the media that I had deeply offended the writer to whom I said "shhh." I was flabbergasted. It had never occurred to me that I had offended this person. I then reflected upon that situation and realized that although I didn't intend to be rude, I could and should have handled the situation much better. I should have said nothing or, at a minimum, politely and privately whispered that the anthem had begun. More than a decade after this incident, I apologized and the person to whom I apologized could not have been more gracious when I did.

Was this the only time I offended someone in the media? I'm quite confident that it was not. I reference it, though, because it's another example of growing up and learning on the job and carrying with me the residue of my mistakes as I did so.

My affirmative decision not to cultivate media relationships for my own benefit also impacted me adversely. When I did interact with the media, I did so for one reason: what I believed to be the good of the organization. I was relatively young when I started with the Raiders and I had no idea that people who worked for teams or for the league office cultivated relationships with the media for their own good, rather than for the good of their employers. It just never occurred to me. Some would say that had nothing to do with my age, that I was simply naïve. But either way – whether due to my youth or naiveté – it was quite a few years before I understood that people did this. No matter, though, as I wouldn't have done so anyway as it's not the right thing to do – even if I had I wanted to, I probably would have sucked at it.

12
COUNTERCLAIM

ANOTHER TOPIC ABOUT WHICH AL AND I DISAGREED WAS THE issue of television blackouts. We argued about this for decades – really, until nearly the end of his life.

Although rules concerning television blackouts are evolving (and although laws related thereto may change), those rules (which dictated that unless a game was sold out 72 hours prior to kickoff, it could not be televised live in the market of the home team) existed throughout my career.

From the outset of my career it was my steadfast view that televising one's games in one's home market is absolutely, positively, unequivocally the single most important marketing tool available to a team. To allow games to be blacked out in one's home market is bad business. Why would an organization want residents of its own market watching other teams? That's dumb. Why would an organization want children in its own market growing up with an affinity for other teams? That's dumb. Organizations shouldn't want and shouldn't allow this to happen and I said it just that clearly to Al: it's dumb.

There existed a number of rules and tools available to clubs so that they could avoid blackouts. Premium seating (club seats, seats in suites) didn't count for purposes of the blackout rule and clubs could adjust manifests to reduce the amount of nonpremium seating so that not every nonpremium seat in the stadium need be sold in order to avoid a blackout. Clubs accomplished this by tarping off large sections of seating or by killing a few seats in each row – a single seat here, a couple of seats there

— in a manner that was unnoticeable to fans and cameras but effective in that thousands fewer seats needed to be sold.

Clubs could also reduce the effective price of a ticket by creatively bundling it with food and beverage, merchandise, or both. Clubs could also offer experiential opportunities or special access with tickets. Clubs could create incentives for local media partners and other business partners to purchase blocks of tickets. Clubs could quiety purchase their own tickets and donate them to charities and community groups if they so desired. There was simply no reason to allow a game to be blacked out and I tried to convince Al of that for many years.

Al vehemently disagreed with me about this and for decades, when the team was in Los Angeles and when it was back in Oakland, we fought about this. Al did not believe that we should have to engage in creative sales efforts to entice fans to purchase tickets. On one particular occasion on which I presented to him some creative, aggressive ticket sales ideas created by the ticket department that we hoped to implement, he responded: "Oh fuck, they [the fans] should just come." I never shared that response with our ticket department.

Most clubs engaged in all sorts of creative marketing initiatives designed to avoid blackouts, a few clubs reduced manifests in large chunks (with tarps), more clubs than most anyone would imagine killed thousands of seats in a manner that was imperceptible, and a fair number of clubs bought their own tickets — all to achieve "sellouts." Al refused to allow us to do such things.

This not only harmed us, it harmed the league as a whole, as it was bad for the league's broadcast partners. To state the obvious, those broadcast partners do not want to black games out, particularly in large markets, such as Los Angeles and the Bay Area. For decades, the league prevailed upon me in every which way to find a way to get our games "sold out," so that they could be televised in our market. I never shared with anyone at the league that we were unable to do so because of the prohibitions Al placed on us. The week of every home game, I dreaded the umpteen calls I would receive from the league on this topic.

Toward the end of his life, when we were having one of our many arguments about this, Al told me that I should do as I wished – not only for the upcoming game but also from that point forward. It struck me as tremendously odd that he not only relented for the upcoming game – which he had done infrequently over the years – but that he relented with respect to all games in the future. I didn't think he was conceding the point because I'd finally convinced him that this was smart business; I thought he was simply tired of arguing with me about it.

I was thrilled to gather a team of employees together and to enlist their help in effectuating this goal. They designed and implemented creative and aggressive marketing strategies and incented sponsors and media partners to work with us to fill the stadium. From that game until I left, only one regular-season game was blacked out.

AL TRUSTED ME. I KNEW that. And I know that people believed that because he trusted me, I could convince him to change his mind. Heck, as noted earlier, there were people who believed that I controlled Al. But as much as Al trusted me, I could rarely change his mind on matters of significance.

There was, though, an issue I believed to be of paramount importance about which I was able to change his mind. It took decades but I eventually convinced him that litigation is not a good business strategy or practice.

Before going further, I want to note that while Al and the Raiders were often perceived as litigious, the team was most often the defendant in the litigation in which we were embroiled. But Al did love to counterclaim with zeal.

One morning, shortly after the news broke that Al had decided to move the team from Los Angeles back to Oakland, I glanced at the *Los*

Angeles Times as I was getting ready to leave for the office. Imagine my surprise when I noticed a short blurb stating the league had filed a lawsuit against us over the impending move. That's how we learned that we had been sued: I read it in the newspaper.

I immediately called our lead lawyer, Jeff, and said: "Have you seen the *Los Angeles Times* this morning?"

Jeff responded a bit impatiently that he had not looked at the paper as he was trying to get ready to leave for the office.

"Well, you'd better look at it now," I said, "because the league filed a lawsuit against us before the court closed last night." So we were the defendants. But we counterclaimed with a vengeance.

A few years later, I again learned of a lawsuit filed against us – in this instance by the City of Oakland and Alameda County and related municipal entities – after it was filed. I was in a meeting in my office when someone walked in with a fax (we used faxes back then) and said, "You'd better look at this." It was a note from a lawyer for the Joint Powers Authority that oversaw and operated the stadium in which we played. The note explained that outside counsel Jeff Kessler would be holding a press conference at City Hall to announce that the city and the county had filed a lawsuit against us. The note stated that the press conference would begin momentarily and as I read it, our phones began ringing like crazy and satellite trucks began pulling into our parking lot. Again we were the defendants, and again, we counterclaimed with a vengeance.

A few years later, while the litigation with both the NFL and the city and county was festering, Al asked me to join him, Jeff Birren, and our outside lawyers at a mandatory court conference. While Al and some of the league and city and county officials were in chambers, representatives of all the parties were in a separate conference room. I was in that room, as was Jeff Kessler. At one point, I turned to him and asked: "Why did you sue us?"

His response was staggering – I will always remember it. In a heavy New York accent, he uttered these words that I can still hear today (accent and all): "Amy, everyone sues to gain leverage in negotiations." For a moment or two, I was speechless and I stared at him with what I was later told by someone in the room was a look of utter incredulity and disgust on my face.

Finally, I said, "Jeff, do you really think that suing Al Davis was the smartest thing to do?"

So, in each of those two instances, the organization was the defendant, not the plaintiff. I'm not sure why, all these years later, even after leaving the organization, I feel such a need to explain that we were the defendant, but we were. I still feel like a kid saying, "But *he* started it."

Some would say that Al's behavior – the organization's behavior, our collective behavior – spurred people to sue us. That's fair to an extent, even if exaggerated or overstated. Certainly, in that era, at a minimum we did not take steps to avoid litigation. And Al sure did like to counterclaim with gusto.

Although I'd tried unsuccessfully for many years to convince Al that it was in our best interest to settle all significant lawsuits (the ones involving the league and the municipalities), I was finally able to do so in the decade before his death, and that was a very satisfying accomplishment.

Al shared with me on a few occasions after we settled the litigation that he only agreed to do so because he understood that it was important to me. He told me that I was the only person who could have convinced him to do so. That was a special moment and it touched me deeply. I told him how much I appreciated that and then I told him if ever he threatened to litigate again, I would chain myself to his leg to prevent it. He looked at me and said: "I believe you."

When he subsequently started making adversarial or litigious noises, I'd remind him of that threat, and we would laugh – but his laugh wasn't gleeful, as was mine; his laugh was mirthless.

13

CHAMPIONSHIP GAME

FOOTBALL GAMES PROVIDE MOMENTS OF SHEER, UTTER JOY
and moments of utter, abject misery.

Game days were exhausting. When we won, they were exhausting and exhilarating and the best days ever. When we lost, they were exhausting and miserable and the worst days ever. After each game, no matter whether we won or we lost, I felt I aged in multiple dog years (more dog years when we lost than when we won). I have long said that I look okay for a woman who is many thousands of years old.

One game that provided moments of absolute ecstasy was the final game of the 1993 season. We were hosting the Denver Broncos, in what for us was a win-and-in game – the Broncos were in the playoffs no matter the outcome.

In the waning moments of the fourth quarter, our season on the line, we were down by seven points (we had been down by 17 points twice in the game). We were inside of the 5-yard line with time for one final play. The ball was snapped and our quarterback, Jeff Hostetler, was looking everywhere for an open receiver. He was looking and looking and looking – he bought time by moving around – it seemed to me that he was looking for an absolute eternity. As I watched, everything slowed down. It was like I was seeing the game in slow motion without any sound at all. I heard nothing, it was absolutely silent. On that final play in regulation, Jeff found Alexander Wright in the corner of the end zone. I saw the ball come out of Jeff's hand. I saw the ball in flight. I saw Alexander leap up and bend backwards, very awkwardly, in what would be his effort to catch it. He had a defender right on him. I saw the ball in Alexander's hands and I realized that he was going to land very awkwardly and very hard. I thought that the moment he hit the ground, the ball might pop out of his hands. Alexander caught the ball and although he landed hard and awkwardly, he held on and we scored. Only then did I hear the noise; it was deafening. Fans were embracing and cheering and screaming and crying. I remember frantically trying to quiet those around me and telling them, "No, no, we're still a point behind, we haven't tied, we haven't done it yet, we still have to kick the extra point." We did.

In overtime, the Broncos won the coin toss and drove right down the field, lickety-splickety. As they were preparing to line up to kick what should have been an easy field goal, I noticed that Pat Bowlen had moved to the sideline. Our crowd was still deafeningly loud. As the Broncos kicker, Jason Elam, approached the ball, I noticed that he took a little, tiny, almost imperceptible stutter step. The kick was up and I saw Pat (PB, as many called him) raise his arms to signal that the kick was good. But it wasn't, Elam missed. We got the ball, drove down the field, kicked the field goal, and won. Elam attributed the fact that he didn't make a clean approach to the ball to the noise of our fans. Home-field advantage.

That touchdown to Wright and winning the game in overtime was sheer, utter ecstasy – a euphoria that is hard to describe. Over 20 years later, I still get chills when thinking about this. I have chills now.

One game that provided moments of abject misery was our 1997 home opener. It was Monday night, September 8, and we were hosting the Chiefs. We were up by less than a touchdown with only a few seconds remaining in the game.

I had gone into the stands to spend some time watching the game with our fans, as I did whenever and as often as I could. I loved the time I spent in the stands with our fans. I never considered that a responsibility or an obligation. I considered it a privilege. In that moment, our fans were ecstatic – they were celebrating, they were sure that we had won this game. I remember repeatedly cautioning the fans with whom I was speaking that "this isn't over" and "the Chiefs can still win this game."

"Don't worry Amy, we won," many fans tried to reassure me. "Don't worry, we got this," they said. I knew that the game was far from over and that we could still lose, and I was terrified.

The Chiefs got the ball back on their 20-yard line with 1:01 remaining. With three seconds left, quarterback Elvis Grbac found wide receiver Andre Rison in the back of the end zone for the touchdown. Rison had gotten behind our defenders and we lost 28–27.

It was one of the most excruciating, most heartbreaking, most painful losses of my career.

A few hours later, I was home, and the phone rang. It was Al. He told me that he was calling to see if I was okay. I was overwhelmed. Al Davis called *me*, to see if *I* was okay. I was thoroughly overwhelmed. His call was more meaningful than he could ever imagine. His call told me that he knew how deeply I cared, how badly I wanted to win, and how devastated I was. It also signaled to me that he cared. He cared enough to call and check on me when he was in misery, too.

JUST AS AL CALLED TO check on me after that devastating Monday-night loss to Kansas City, he once called me to revel in a particularly delicious victory.

It was December 2008 and for differing reasons, neither Al nor I traveled to Tampa Bay for the season finale. I watched the game at home with my husband. Well, I was home with my husband and we both watched the game, but we didn't watch the whole game together. I wasn't an easy person with whom to watch a game. It was often better that I watched by myself, and we both understood that.

We were down by 10 points in the fourth quarter but went on to win. Michael Bush had 177 yards rushing, 129 of which came in the fourth quarter. We knocked the Buccaneers out of the playoff race.

The moment the game ended, the phone rang. I knew it would be someone calling about the game. I never for a minute thought it would be Al, but it was. He called chortling, to relish in and share the moment with me, which touched me deeply.

I periodically opted out of traveling with the team to one road game each December. I remained back to work on year-end matters. I tried to select a game that was a two-day trip so I could enjoy and capitalize on the quiet of the office once the team left on Friday and again on Saturday. I watched those games from home. My husband and I never let anyone watch with us – this wasn't for fun, this wasn't relaxed viewing, and I didn't allow talking during the game, not even during the commercials. It was my rule that only I was allowed to make or elicit a comment about or during the game. I was no fun during games. My husband and I would initially watch together, but it was a certainty that at some point very soon after the game began, watching together would come to an abrupt end. I would leave the room and we would watch from different spots from that point on. My husband always said that any decision to watch from different rooms would be mine, but I know that he was relieved when I would retreat to a far point in the house.

My husband also looked out for the neighbors. In one instance, this occurred when the team was in Pittsburgh to play the Steelers on December 6, 2009. As it was a December game across the country, I had elected to stay back.

We scored three late touchdowns, the final one with nine seconds to go – it was Louis Murphy's second touchdown in a five-and-a-half-minute period. I watched that drive leading to that final winning touchdown, standing on the bed screaming at the television – every curse word I knew, and some I didn't know I knew, spewing from my mouth.

I am sure that I resembled Linda Blair in *The Exorcist* – the part where her head spins around in circles and green vomit shoots from her mouth. My husband walked upstairs from where he had been watching the game (at the television in the part of the house farthest from me), entered the bedroom, and calmly and silently began closing all of the windows. So, we got to watch the final, winning drive together, as I was standing on the bed screaming and cursing at the television like a crazy person, and as he was closing all the windows. After we won, I asked him why he would spend time closing windows during those final thrilling moments of the game. He responded that he had done so because he didn't want to have to spend the rest of the day explaining to the police that although the neighbors may have reported a murder or a hostage situation, it was simply me, watching a game.

I ALWAYS LOVED SPENDING TIME with our fans. Whether in the parking lots before the games, in the stands during the games, at home or on the road, I loved it. It was important to me, it was fun, it was special, it was a highlight of my career. I considered this a real privilege – not a responsibility or an obligation, but a privilege.

The president of a division rival once asked me in a scornful tone: "Why do you always do that? Why do you always go through the stands, talking to all the fans?"

He went on to say that he had seen me do this at our home games and when we were in his stadium. As disdainful as he was, he was also sincerely curious. He just didn't understand why I did this. I responded by asking: "Why wouldn't I spend time with our fans? I love to do that. Why don't you do that with your fans?" He didn't answer. I didn't stop spending time in the stands. He didn't start.

Seeing and interacting with fans at games confirmed my views about the power of sports. There can and should be reasonable debate about the role of sports in our communities and about the level of commitment, if any, that municipalities and states should make with respect to sports venues. We should engage in discussions about whether public money should be used for stadiums and arenas, whether sports organizations should be subsidized in this manner, whether expenditure on infrastructure surrounding stadiums and arenas is a good investment, whether stadiums and arenas are environmentally appropriate, and more. Reasonable minds may differ, but these topics should be debated.

I do not believe, however, that the powerful, unifying impact that sports has on communities is open to debate.

For almost 30 years, at every game I saw people who might otherwise never interact with one another embrace in moments of joy and commiserate with one another in moments of despair.

To see men and women of all races, ethnicities, ages, religions, socioeconomic strata, and political persuasions erupt in collective ecstasy and embrace in utter jubilation was very powerful. When I saw people who may never have believed that they had anything in common with one another share moments and experiences together in a stadium, it was my thought and my hope that they would realize that they actually did share at least something in common and that this realization would permeate other parts of their lives.

Perhaps the next time a disagreement, a dispute, or a conflict arose, the octogenarian who lived in a rural area and the teenager who lived in the inner city might recall the instance in which they embraced and they both might understand that people do have, and can find, more in common than they might otherwise have believed.

The value of that can't be quantified.

VERY EARLY IN MY CAREER, I was told in no uncertain terms not to "act cold" when around the team (whether on the practice field or on the playing field prior to a game), no matter how cold I was. No hands in pockets, no arms around oneself, no suggestions or hints by body language or otherwise that one was cold. Al didn't want anyone to act cold, he explained, as he thought that if we acted cold, the players would then – and only then – realize that it was cold. *Okay, that's dumb*, I thought. People know when it's cold; they don't need to be told that it's cold to know it's cold. But I was careful not to act cold – even if I was freezing.

We were in Green Bay to play a game on December 26, 1993, and it was cold – really, really, bone-chillingly cold – a veritable polar vortex by my standards. At one point, and perhaps still, the Packers website listed that game as the fourth-coldest game ever played at Lambeau Field. The wind chill was minus-22 degrees. I can't fathom what games No. 1 through No. 3 on that list must have been like. Certainly, that day was the coldest I had ever been and that remains the case to this day.

Wearing what constituted my winter clothes, I had only to make it from the lobby of the hotel to the team bus and then from the team bus to the visiting team staff seating area in the press box. As I started out the door of the hotel, I was blasted by the cold, but I kept my coat over my arm, so as not to "act as if" I was cold. As I walked out the door in my lightweight sweater and slacks, a player shouted from the bus: "Amy, put on your fucking coat; we know it's cold!"

The new reality that a woman now traveled with a team came into focus on that cold day. Just behind our staff seating area was a restroom – the sort of restroom that accommodates one person at a time – and that therefore had no gender demarcation on the door. Before kickoff, I used that restroom without incident.

At the break between the first and second quarters, I tried to use it again. As I approached, a guard standing beside the restroom shifted his position to the front of the door, and said, "Men's room." I looked at him. *Huh?* "No, it's not," I said. "It's for everyone."

"Men's room," he responded. I explained that I had just used that restroom right before kickoff. "Men's room," he responded.

"Sir," I said, "only one person can use it at a time."

"Men's room," he stated.

"It doesn't have a 'men's room' sign on the door," I countered.

"Men's room," he intoned. I wasn't going to win this argument. I needed to use the restroom and the second quarter was about to start. So I asked him where, precisely, I should go to use a restroom. I listened in disbelief as he explained that I had to go outside, walk to an upper deck, and use the public restroom there. I wasn't at all bothered by the prospect of using a public restroom – I did that all the time in stadiums and, as noted earlier, believed that it was important to do so. It was the going outside part that stunned me. I walked outside, went upstairs, and found a restroom. It had walls and a roof, but the walls didn't reach or join the roof; they stopped about two feet below it. As I used the restroom, my only thought was that I might very well freeze to death and none of my coworkers would know where I was.

IN THE DAYS LEADING UP to a game, and on game day itself, weather was a topic I discussed quite frequently with Al. I learned very early in my career – about the time I started exploring the organization (literally and figuratively), that I should always know the weather forecast for our upcoming game. Starting on Wednesday, he would often ask me, "What's the weather?" I knew what he meant was: "What's the weather going to be on game day?" Had I responded, "Let me look that up," or "I don't know, I'll check," he would never have asked me again. So, I made sure to know the weather forecast for each upcoming game. I'd check it frequently so that no matter when he called, I'd have a current forecast, and also because I was interested.

Al would frequently call me at home on the morning of home game days. He was very tense, as I was, and he was curt. He would express anger about something that he had heard or read; he would express frustration or disappointment that a certain player couldn't play (or "go," as is said in the business); he'd want to know who was singing the anthem, the anticipated weather at kickoff, or some other detail about game day.

I was extraordinarily tense on game days. My husband likened me on game-day mornings to a "hummingbird on speed." When I shared that with a colleague at another club, she laughed and told me that her husband likened her on game-day mornings to a "cat on crack."

On one occasion, Al called me at home early on a really rainy, stormy game-day morning and asked me to call the president of the visiting team at his hotel and get him to agree that we delay kickoff. *Huh?* "Teams can't delay kickoff," I told him. "The networks pay a lot of money to televise the games and we can't just change the time of kickoff." He wasn't impressed. "Try to get kickoff delayed," he instructed me, and hung up. We kicked off in the rain and the storm.

THE SAME SEASON IN WHICH I made my first road trip with the team, we advanced to the AFC championship game. Roughly a month after that, Al told me to come into his office to "work on playoff bonuses." I didn't know what that meant. Playoff bonuses for players are collectively bargained and thus standard throughout the league. Sometimes, a coach or a general manager has a playoff bonus clause in his contract. Nonplayer bonuses and bonuses for those to whom the organization is not contractually obligated are left up to the discretion of owners (or someone to whom the owner delegates such decisions).

I joined Al in his office and he handed me a copy of a staff list he had front of him. He read down the list, and as he said each name aloud, he stated the amount he planned to give each person. At this point in my career, he didn't want any input from me; he simply wanted me to implement his decision. When he came to my name, he stated an amount I was to receive. I was shocked. I was speechless. Never – never in a zillion years – did I think I would receive a playoff bonus. That I was included in Al's thoughts was worth more to me than any amount of bonus.

When I shared this news with my husband, he suggested that we use that unexpected bonus to purchase a horse that I had been riding and had fallen in love with. So we did. And since we were only able to do so because of this playoff bonus, I chose Championship Game as his show name. A number of years later, when we (the horse and I) hit a really bad patch preparing for and in competitions, my husband dryly asked: "Did it ever occur to you that naming a horse after a game you lost by 48 points might not have been such a good idea?"

14

IT WAS A FUMBLE

ON JANUARY 13, 1991, WE HOSTED THE CINCINNATI BENGALS in a divisional playoff game. I was standing on the rooftop of the press box when Bo Jackson was pulled down by his leg on the far sideline. There was no violent hit or tackle, and it didn't appear that Bo was hurt. As he was pulled down, we could see that his leg twisted at the hip, but it did not appear to be the sort of tackle that would lead to an injury. Even as Bo lay there, and we realized that he was injured on the play, we didn't have a sense the injury was devastating.

Bo did not play the next week in the AFC championship game in Buffalo, and he never played another down in the NFL. He had suffered a career-ending injury.

There's great truth to an adage I learned very early in my career: *coulda, shoulda, and woulda never played a down*. Injuries are part of the game and it's a frustrating waste of time and energy to think about what coulda, shoulda, or woulda happened had Bo not suffered that injury. There's no doubt, though, that we would have been an entirely different team for years to come with a healthy Bo Jackson.

I REMEMBER CERTAIN DETAILS ABOUT almost every game we played during my nearly three decades with the team – both the wins and the losses, the ecstasy and the heartbreak.

One of my favorite plays in one of my favorite games was 25 Bingo Cross.

On October 11, 1998, we hosted the San Diego Chargers. Our starting quarterback, Jeff George, was injured. We began the game with Donald Hollas at quarterback, but in the fourth quarter we pulled him and put in 39-year-old Wade Wilson.

We didn't have a first down in the third quarter. (Neither did the Chargers, by the way.) Our punter, Leo Araguz, punted 16 times in the game and, collectively, the punters for both teams set what was then a record for punting yards. With roughly two minutes left in the game, we were trailing 6–0. With a bit more than a minute and a half remaining in the game, Wade Wilson threw to a wide-open James Jett, who had flown down the field and right by the corner who was (not really) covering him. It appeared to me that in order to get the ball to James, Wade jumped on his tippy toes and put every ounce of his body and his weight into that throw. We scored and we won 7–6.

So many people – fans, media, analysts – decried the game for its woeful lack of offense. I had a different perspective. I thought it was – and still think it is – a defensive masterpiece.

WE WERE IN KANSAS CITY for the final regular-season game of the 1999 season, which was actually to be played on January 2, 2000. That morning, while flipping through a local newspaper in the hotel restaurant, I read a column that really annoyed me. The premise of the column was that the Chiefs were in the playoffs and the writer assessed potential playoff matchups and the Chiefs' prospects. Well, the Chiefs had not yet clinched a playoff berth; they needed to beat us to do so. The columnist dismissively acknowledged this a few paragraphs later, noting that although the Chiefs weren't yet in the playoffs and must win that day to get in, they were playing the Raiders, so victory was a certainty. The column then went back to analyzing the Chiefs' chances in the playoffs.

I was indignant. I was all riled up.

I grabbed the paper, stormed off to our team buses, and shoved the paper – folded open to this column – toward a member of the equipment staff and asked him to post it in the locker room at Arrowhead Stadium.

In the first quarter, the Chiefs returned both a punt and an interception for touchdowns and we were down 17–0. Obviously, one never wants to start any game like that, but falling behind like that in Arrowhead was a particular nightmare. For almost my entire career I considered Arrowhead one of the two loudest outdoor stadiums in the league, the other being Buffalo. That remained the case until the new stadium in Seattle was built, at which time that venue joined Kansas City and Buffalo atop the list of the loudest outdoor venues.

It was cacophonous that day in Arrowhead. I likened games like that to a shark feeding frenzy – both the players and fans reminded me of sharks who had smelled blood in the water. It was always deafeningly loud, but during games like this it was even louder.

Finally, with a bit of time remaining in the first quarter, we blocked a punt, Kenny Shedd scooped it up, and we scored.

A lot is said about momentum. Momentum is tangible; it is palpable. It swings, it shifts, it is real, and it matters.

That blocked punt, returned for a touchdown, shifted the momentum. We soon led 21–17. As the game continued, we traded the lead several times. One touchdown, dubbed the Run of the Millennium, remains one of my favorite plays of my career.

Kansas City was leading 31–28. Rich Gannon handed the ball to one of my all-time favorite running backs, Tyrone Wheatley. Tyrone broke seven tackles (although it seemed to be three times as many) and carried what looked like all 11 defenders into the end zone. That touchdown put us up 35–31.

Ultimately, the game went into overtime and we won by a field goal. No playoff berth for the Chiefs. I had never, ever heard Arrowhead Stadium so quiet. It was delightfully, deliciously quiet – one really could have heard the proverbial pin drop. I wanted to run through the stadium singing "Oh

What a Beautiful Morning," but I didn't. There are few things worse in sport than an obnoxious winner. But I sure did want to sing that day.

ANOTHER OF MY FAVORITE RUNNING plays helped put us in the Super Bowl.

It was January 19, 2003, and we were hosting the Tennessee Titans in the AFC Championship Game. We traded the lead for a period of time and the final score does not reflect how close the game was.

Less than five minutes into the game, we scored, but I had a sense that this was a game in which the lead would go back and forth, a lot. Shortly after we scored, I walked through the area in which my husband was sitting with some family and friends. They were cheering and celebrating our touchdown, they were jubilant, ebullient. It seemed to me that they were behaving as if we had won the game. I looked at my husband and, shaking with anger and from nerves, I'm sure, said: "These people are acting like this is fun." *These people* referred, of course, to our family and dear friends. Clearly, I was even more tense than was normally the case during a game. My husband gently steered me away and said, "Maybe it would be better if you didn't stop by and see us at all during this game." Indeed.

In the fourth quarter, Zack Crockett was lined up as the single back. Everyone in the stadium knew that Zack would get the ball and that we would run a play we had run successfully all year – 12 Blast. Our fans knew what was coming and the Titans knew what was coming, but the Titans couldn't stop us. Zack scored and at that moment I knew; we were going to the Super Bowl.

I was standing alone, watching the end of the game from a corner in the very back of our Spanish-language radio broadcast booth. The play-by-play announcer and color commentator were in the front of the booth doing their jobs, while I clung to a wall in the back, alone. I had hidden myself there in the waning moments of the game.

That moment was the best moment of my career. One week later was the worst.

ANOTHER OF MY FAVORITE RUNNING plays involved a running back less well known than Marcus, Bo, Tyrone, or Zack. We were hosting the New York Jets on October 10, 1993, and we were down 20–17, with almost no time left. We had time for possibly one more play. Coaches and players were signaling frantically for Vince Evans to spike the ball. Vince saw them, ignored them, and ran a play. He handed the ball to Nick Bell on the 1-yard line, and Nick scored. We won the game on that final play.

Just before that play, as the team was breaking the huddle and approaching the line of scrimmage, Vince grabbed Nick and said something to him. After the game, Vince was asked by the media what he said to Nick, and he told them that he said, "Run, Nick, run." I was a bit dubious about that, so a bit later I asked Vince whether that was, in fact, what he had said to Nick. It was not. Vince told me that what he really said was: "If you don't get in the fucking end zone, don't come back to the locker room."

IN EACH OF THE TWO seasons before we went to the Super Bowl in January 2003, we were also in the playoffs. In January 2001 we lost the AFC Championship Game to the Baltimore Ravens and in January 2002, well, that playoff game was in New England.

For much of the game against the Ravens, we played without our starting quarterback Rich Gannon, who had suffered an injury when Tony Siragusa landed – actually, flopped – on him. Losing Rich in the second quarter and then a really bad pursuit angle resulted in a loss. The pain of losing and of knowing that we would not advance to the Super Bowl was excruciating. Knowing that another team would accept the Lamar Hunt

AFC Championship Trophy on our field was gut-wrenching. I didn't watch.

January 19, 2002: the divisional playoff game. New England. The Tuck Rule. It was a fumble.

Raiders fans, football fans, sports fans – they all know or they know of the Tuck Rule Game. For those people who don't, this is what happened: with less than two minutes remaining in the game, Charles Woodson forced a Tom Brady fumble, which Greg Biekert recovered. That fumble recovery meant that we won the game. We would have kneeled down three times and gone home.

I was watching the game from the visiting staff area in the New England press box. Cheering was not allowed in the press box, so when Charles forced that fumble and Greg recovered it, we celebrated as silently as we could – we grabbed one another, we squeezed one another's shoulders, we hugged one another, we clasped one another's hands. We had won the game.

A moment or so after the play, I realized it was under review. Because the play had been run with less than two minutes remaining in the game, the review was initiated by league officials. That fact alone dictated the outcome of the game. Had the play occurred even one second prior to the two-minute warning, the game would have been over, as any challenge to the ruling on the field would have had to come from New England and because New England was out of timeouts they could not have challenged the play. So, it would have remained our ball, we would have kneeled down three times, game over.

It is said that football is a game of inches and a game of seconds. It is, indeed.

Years later, a *Sports Illustrated* article recounted that when I learned that the play was to be reviewed, I turned to the approximately 80-year-old director of officiating and said: "You'd better call 911, because I'm going to have a fucking heart attack if you overturn this fucking call."

Well, when that article was published, I asked my husband in an indignant tone of voice: "I didn't say that – did I say that? No, I didn't say that. Did I? You were sitting right next to me, did I say that?"

"No," he responded, "you didn't say that."

Well, now I was even more indignant. "I knew I didn't say that…I'm calling *Sports Illustrated*," I declared.

"Before you do that," my husband replied, "let me tell you what you did say. You said, 'You'd better call 911, because I'm going to have a fucking stroke if you overturn this fucking call.'"

Oh. I said *stroke*, not heart attack. I didn't call *Sports Illustrated*.

That *Sports Illustrated* article also referred to me by a nickname: the Princess of Darkness. I'm often asked if I'm offended by that name. Offended? I love that name. I cherish that name. I am deeply honored by it and I shall embrace it proudly, always.

A few days after the game, I asked Al which was worse – the Tuck Rule or the Lytle Fumble. The latter refers to Rob Lytle, who played for the Denver Broncos. In the 1978 AFC Championship game, Lytle was hit by Raiders great Jack Tatum, the ball popped out, and it was recovered by a linebacker, who started running the other way. It was going to be a touchdown but the officials ruled Lytle's forward progress had stopped before the ball came loose, and the whistle was blown. I wanted to know which hurt more, or if these things could be quantified.

Al considered my question for a bit, and responded: "Right now, I'd have to say this one," and then he paused, and added, "but only because it's more recent."

Whenever I write or speak publicly about that fumble, I receive immediate feedback telling me to "get over it." But that's the fun of sports – we don't have to get over these sorts of things. We have to get over all sorts of things in life, but not in sports.

And it was a fumble.

ONCE AL MADE A DECISION – WHETHER I AGREED WITH IT OR not – it was my responsibility to make the best of that decision. In those instances in which I disagreed with him, I did so prospectively and directly, before the decision was made. When I failed at my efforts to change his mind it was my job to turn his decision into the best decision it could be. I also believed that it was my responsibility to keep confidential the fact that I disagreed with a decision. It was neither right nor appropriate, in my view, to let it be known outside of the organization that I thought Al was wrong or that I disagreed with his decision. Once a decision was made, I proceeded as if it was the decision of the organization.

There are employees who don't express disagreement before a decision is made, but who, after it is, whisper to the media, colleagues, and others that it wasn't their decision or that they didn't agree with it.

They do this in an effort to distance themselves from decisions in order to protect their own reputations, all the while taking a paycheck from the same owner and organization they are undermining. I didn't respect that. I thought that if one disagreed, one should do so prospectively and directly in an effort to affect a decision, not to later distance oneself from it.

In 2009, we drafted Darrius Heyward-Bey. As is often the case in the weeks and days leading up to the draft, there are leaks, and the media predicts whom a team will select. This prospective draft pick was resoundingly and harshly criticized. It was condemned as a "typical Al Davis pick."

(By way of note, Darrius was at all times a tremendous teammate. He was proud to be a Raider. It certainly was not his doing that we drafted him as high as we did, opprobrium should not have been directed at him, and he handled the situation maturely and magnificently.)

Just moments before it was our turn to draft, Al had someone who was with him in the draft room locate me. I was never in the draft room at any time during my career and in this instance I was downstairs entertaining our guests – civic leaders, sponsors, suite holders, business partners. The individual who located me instructed me to head to a phone in a private area, away from our guests, as Al wished to speak with me. "Trask, we're going to take him," he said. "It's going to be hard on you, we'll get hit, you'll have to handle it."

And then he hung up and I went back to our guests.

When Al said "we'll get hit," this was his acknowledgement that we would be excoriated by the media, analysts, and others. When Al told me "you'll have to handle it," I knew what he meant. I would have to mollify our fans, ticket holders, suite holders, advertisers, sponsors, and business partners. Even knowing what was to come, I smiled wryly as I noted Al's choice of words: "You'll have to handle it."

I wasn't surprised by that choice of words – that was Al's view; that I'd have to handle it. I was, however, surprised by his recognition and acknowledgment that there would be adverse consequences to his decision. Al rarely acknowledged that we would be harshly criticized for our actions or inactions. In fact, I can recall only one other instance during my career in which he did so. Further, Al never believed that such criticism would impact our business and admonished me for suggesting that it would.

He told me that I'd have to handle it. He was right, it was my job.

IN 2008, AL PUBLICLY ACCUSED the New England Patriots of tampering with Randy Moss. But they didn't. A Raiders employee initiated discussions with the Patriots about Moss and the Patriots engaged in a dialogue, but they did not tamper. I explained that to Al but, to use one of his favorite phrases, he didn't "see it that way" and he told the press that the Patriots had tampered. The Patriots were understandably incensed and a league employee informed me that they had indicated intent to file a tampering claim against us.

Shortly after Al publicly leveled those tampering accusations, I attended a league meeting. Prior to the start of the meeting, I searched for Robert Kraft, the owner of the New England Patriots, because I wanted to broach the issue of Al's comments with him and to apologize to him and his organization. When I found him, it was quite evident that he was very angry and my distinct impression was that he would refuse to speak with me. But he did speak with me. He listened to me, he engaged in a conversation, and he responded in an understanding, gracious, and generous manner. The result of that conversation: no grievance, no litigation.

Someone once said to me that litigation signifies failure. I think that is wise and powerful, and I agree with that as a general rule. In my experience, admitting when one is wrong, engaging in an open, honest dialogue and apologizing are often all that's required to avoid litigation.

Very early in my career, I also acknowledged that we did something wrong, I apologized, and we avoided litigation in that instance as well.

It was 1989 and we had named Art Shell as our head coach. Our merchandise and promotions staff quickly produced hats and shirts emblazoned with the words "Shell's Angels" atop a logo that was obviously very similar to the Hells Angels logo. Almost immediately thereafter, I received a letter from the law firm representing the Hells Angels. That firm was (and still is) one of the most respected law firms in the country. My first thought when I received the letter was, *Holy crap, the Hells Angels sure don't mess around when it comes to legal counsel.*

The letter stated in no uncertain terms that we had violated the intellectual property rights of the Hells Angels. They were right – we did.

Rather than sending back a "lawyer letter" in which I endeavored to justify our conduct, saber rattle, or posture, I picked up the phone and called the firm that had sent the letter. I said two things to the lawyer with whom I spoke: "You are right," and "We are sorry." The lawyer was silent for what seemed to be a long time. I assumed that was because he was surprised by my admission of wrongdoing and my apology – those aren't typical responses to such a letter. Ultimately, a lawyer from the firm called me back and explained that their client appreciated our apology and wished for us to sell what we had in stock but not produce any more. Wow. I was stunned. It would have been entirely customary and appropriate for them to demand that we destroy what we had in stock. That was what I had hoped would be the response: destroy it and we won't sue you. Instead, the Hells Angels suggested that we sell what we had.

The lawyer noted that the Hells Angels appreciated the apology I offered and didn't want us to suffer economic harm. Wow.

Sometimes, acknowledging that one is wrong and apologizing solves a lot of problems. Saying "I am sorry" matters. I told Robert Kraft that we were wrong and that I was sorry. But I still believe – and always will – that it was a fumble.

IN MEETINGS AND DISCUSSIONS WITH others on staff, I often analogized our business to the human body – there are parts one wants the public to see and parts one does not want the public to see. Our tax, finance, banking, legal, and compliance work were, I explained, analogous to internal organs – the kidney, the liver, the spleen – parts of the body one hopes are never seen. Our community, social media, Internet, broadcast, and fan engagement work were analogous to extremities and facial features – arms, hands, fingers, eyes, ears – parts of the body the public will see, that we want the public to see. I enjoyed working on both.

Some people think that finance and banking work is dull and find it odd that I enjoyed it as much as I did. It was one of my favorite parts of my job. I loved it because it was interesting, complex, challenging, and of intrinsic importance to the organization, and because I had the privilege of working with remarkable people.

I worked with a phenomenal lawyer who is one of the smartest people I have ever met and who I believe is one of the best lawyers in the world. I called him innumerable times – often at crazy hours – with a very direct request, which I often stated in a pleading tone: "Help me."

I am never hesitant to acknowledge when I need help, and I am never hesitant to enlist those best suited to provide it. Had I failed to do so, it would have been a disservice to the organization. Seeking help from those who are smarter, had greater expertise, or were more capable than me of solving a problem strikes me as obvious and ethical. It never ceases to amaze me when people opt not to do that. Rather than shying away from enlisting help from those better able to provide it, I eagerly did so.

The gentleman to whom I referred above did just that – he helped me and he helped our business. He made me and he made us far better than I or we would otherwise have been. That's what good teammates do – they make one another other better. If the left tackle is having trouble blocking his man, the guard beside him will handle his man and also help the tackle with his, as teammates working toward a common goal should.

I also worked with a terrific banking lawyer and I relied upon her to help me and to help our business and she did just that. This work was complicated and crucial and she too made me better than I otherwise would have been.

We had fantastic bankers who knew and cared about our business. Together, we fashioned creative solutions to a host of considerable challenges. I relied upon these individuals to help me problem solve in every way, so much so that I was acting instinctively when, during a game, I grabbed the arm of one of our bankers and pleaded with him: "*Do something.*"

We were in Tennessee and we were letting the game slip away – we really needed to make a play to seal a victory. I was frantic and grabbed the banker who had accompanied us as our guest and who was sitting next to me, and I beseeched him to "do something." My request probably sounded like a cross between a whine and a wail. Well, on the very next play, we forced a turnover. We won. I turned to him and said: "Now *that* is full-service banking."

I knew that there was nothing our banker could help us do to win that game. My request for him to "do something" was utterly instinctive on my part. I routinely requested all sorts of assistance from individuals who provided it spectacularly and without fail, so it was natural to ask for help.

Our bankers also helped me replace lipstick that I had managed to lose on the team charter from Oakland to Charlotte. On Saturday morning, I dragged them to a drug store so that I could purchase a new one. Why am I recounting this story? Am I proud or bragging that I dragged the organization's bankers with as I shopped for lipstick? No.

I shared this story because while one might think that the last thing a businesswoman should do is ask men who bank the business for which she works to join her on a lipstick run, it never occurred to me that so doing would affect our working relationship and it didn't. In fact, as I perused the collection of available lipstick, our bankers jumped right in, sharing with me their thoughts about the best color. Once again, full-service banking.

My experiences throughout my career suggest to me that some accepted truisms aren't always true.

Tremendous lawyers and full-service bankers notwithstanding, it was a challenge to work with Al on financial issues. Okay, it was a challenge to work with Al on a lot of issues, but working with Al on banking matters was especially difficult.

You see, banking agreements contain covenants and commitments, and Al rarely accepted any constraints – banking, league, or otherwise – on the manner in which he chose to do business.

I repeatedly explained our responsibilities and the commitments we had made. I was clear. I was explicit. He would acknowledge that he heard me and that he understood me, and then he would go on to do precisely as he pleased without regard to what I had communicated. Again and again, I would remind him of our contractual obligations. It didn't help. On one occasion on which I reminded him of a central covenant in our agreements, he responded by saying: "Oh fuck, you're the only one in the world who makes that a big deal." Yes Al, I'm the only one in the world who thinks EBITDA (earnings before interest, taxes, depreciation, and amortization) is a big deal. Good to know.

When Al knew that I was working on a banking or financial matter, he would check in with me periodically and ask, "How are you coming with your little problem?" My little problem? First of all, these weren't "my" problems, they were our problems, organizational problems, and they weren't "little" problems; they were really big problems. But Al really did believe that financial and banking issues were my problems, and to my great relief and appreciation, he generally left me alone to work on them with the legal and banking experts I gathered to assist us, which was distinctly different than in other areas of our business. I think – and I hope – that this was because he knew that he could count on me to handle these matters. Once, while we were in the midst of a particularly stressful banking transaction, I asked Al, "How come you're not up all night, every night, unable to sleep, worried about this like I am?" He responded: "I have you to do that for me." That actually made me feel good.

It was very meaningful – very significant – to me that Al trusted me and relied upon me to figure these things out. I remember his tone of voice when he said, "God bless you, little girl," after I shared with him that I had found a solution to a big problem. That remark meant more to me than any salary could.

Clubs are required to provide a tremendous amount of financial information to the league office. At varying times throughout the year, clubs provide a number of audited reports, financial statements, projections, forecasts, analysis, and more. Clubs are also required to meet with the league office on a periodic basis to discuss that material and to respond to league inquiries.

During these meetings, as I sat there listening to league executives raise questions and concerns about the state of our finances and league financial issues, I thought how fun it would have been to see the expressions on their faces if they had heard Al tell me that I was the only person in the world who thinks that EBITDA is a big deal.

SOMEONE FOR WHOM I HAVE tremendous respect once told me, "You need to have a five-year plan." He was not suggesting a five-year plan for the Raiders, but a five-year "Amy plan." My response: "What the fuck am I, Russia? I don't need a five-year plan." I did not have a five-year plan when I took my job and I didn't have one at any time while working for the organization. I don't have a five-year plan now.

I want to be very clear: I do believe that businesses should engage in long-term, strategic planning. In the last years of Al's life the organization made – and failed to make – some decisions that suggested that we weren't engaging in long-term, strategic planning – or, if we were, we weren't doing it well. Those are fair observations and criticisms in some regards. Although I never responded or otherwise commented at the time, I did note to a few people after Al passed away that when someone is older and in poor health, long-term has a different meaning than when one is younger and in good health. Most of us can but imagine what it is like to confront one's own mortality, let alone run a business knowing that for us, long-term was not particularly long.

So, although I do believe that businesses should have long-term, strategic plans, I didn't want nor have one for myself. I still don't want one and I still don't have one. There is no "Amy plan."

Besides, as I reminded the person close to me who suggested that I should have one: that the whole five-year-plan thing didn't work out so well for Russia.

I MENTIONED EARLIER THAT I once quit my job.

I was furious with Al. I was livid. And he was as angry with me as he had ever been.

Our disagreement on this subject came to a head on a Monday morning in September, the day after we had lost a game on the road.

We were on the phone and again, the topic of a prospective coaching change arose. It was one of our more vicious arguments and finally, furious and frustrated, I said: "Well, I resign."

"Okay, alright, you resign, fine," Al said. "You can resign in January."

"Perhaps you didn't understand me," I responded, "I just quit...I don't work for you anymore, so you can't tell me when I can resign, because I just did."

As we were screaming at one another, I sent an email to my husband explaining that I had just quit my job and that he needed to come to the office. I wanted him there. Just as I concluded my phone call with Al, my husband arrived. We sat in my office. I was stunned and shaking – we didn't speak. A fellow staff member with whom I worked very closely joined us. We all just stared at one another and barely spoke and then I went home. I was a wreck all night. I'd just quit my job – a job I loved.

The next morning, I got up and started getting ready in the manner I did every day. My husband asked me what I was doing and when I responded in a very matter-of-fact manner – as if nothing was out of the ordinary – that I was going to the office, he dryly stated: "Perhaps this fact escapes you, but you quit your job yesterday; you have no office."

But I went to the office and I sat at my desk, working. At roughly 10:00 AM, the phone rang. It was Al. In one of his warmest, nicest tones, he asked about a few projects that he knew were important to me, offered his input and assistance, and volunteered to do something that he'd previously refused to do.

I had been trying for quite some time to convince Al to give an on-camera interview for an ESPN 30 for 30 project (*Straight Outta L.A.*) that

Ice Cube was directing, but Al had been steadfast in his refusal to do so. In this nice, warm tone, Al asked when I'd like him to get together with "(my) friend Ice Cube" for the interview. The second I hung up, I called and made the arrangements, before he could change his mind. Al and I never, ever spoke of the fact that I had quit.

I MENTION MY HUSBAND QUITE a bit throughout this book – but I don't mention him by name. That is because he might seek a cease-and-desist order if I did. Of course, I'm teasing – he wouldn't actually do that, I don't think, but he did once tell me that he might do so.

I was working on a project at home, and I left our media guide out on the kitchen counter. He picked it up and, as he was flipping through it, saw that his name was in it. The guide stated something to this effect: Trask is married. Her husband's name is ____. (Only there wasn't a blank, it actually said his name.) As innocuous as that reference was, he didn't like it. So, he very humorously stated that he intended to seek a cease-and-desist order prohibiting us from including his name in future years. (We never did again include his name in the media guide.)

So, without using his name, I'll share a story.

When Al decided to move the team from Los Angeles back to Oakland, I was overwhelmed by the amount of work to be done. After one particularly stressful and long day, I arrived home at about 1:30 AM and woke my husband to share with him that I had too much to do, that I couldn't get it all done, and that I was panicked. He looked at me like I was dense and said: "Then why are you home? If that's the case, you should be at the office." He didn't coddle me; he didn't suggest that it was unreasonable of anyone to expect me to work that hard; he didn't complain that I was, in essence, living at the office. He led me to our kitchen, we ate a snack, and then he saw me off to the office at two in the morning.

My husband encouraged and helped me in every way imaginable throughout my career and he continues to encourage and to help me in every way imaginable now.

I am often told, "Your husband is so supportive." "No, he's not," I respond. Of course, that response always engenders surprised looks. I then explain that to describe him simply as supportive is an insulting understatement. Look, supportive is good – supportive is terrific – and many people would love to have a partner who is supportive. But my husband was and is so much more than supportive. He encourages me and he rolls up his sleeves to help me in every possible way. My husband believes in me when I don't believe in myself. He believes that I can accomplish things when I am not entirely sure that I can. He inspires me and makes me strive to be the very best I can be.

Many times throughout my career, many people – fans, media, those with whom I interacted in business – shared with me that it was their impression that the Raiders were "my life" and that I cared more about the Raiders than I cared about anything else.

I loved being a Raider. Being a Raider dominated our lives for almost three decades and we loved that it did. During that time, it defined our schedule and created our routines; our lives revolved around football and around the Raiders.

I never wanted to celebrate the New Year on January 1; I considered the day after the Super Bowl, when every team went back to 0–0 to be the first day of the New Year. My favorite day between the end of one season and the start of the next was the day the schedule was announced. I absolutely loved schedule release day and was a dork about it. Each year I called a meeting – it was an annual rite of spring – and asked every business operations employee to engage in all sorts of schedule guessing games. I created spreadsheets with the schedules of each team in our division, our conference, and the league as a whole. I loved that day.

For months leading up to the start of the season, I would anticipate that moment when the kicker's foot would make contact with the ball on the first play of the first game and the first game of the season would be underway. No matter where in the stadium I was, I could hear – or at least I imagined that I could hear – the sound of his foot on the ball. That is a magical moment. I eagerly anticipated that same moment of each game. I never slept the night before games.

Games are full of magical moments. Some plays seem to be in slow motion; some plays are like the most magnificent ballet; some plays seem to happen at the speed of light. I always likened games to snowflakes – no two are the same.

The Raiders were indescribably important to me and I cared about the organization more than I believe anyone will ever understand. I loved being a Raider; I was proud to be a Raider. But all of that said, nothing has ever been or will be as important to me as my husband. I care about him more than anything. That surprises some people, but not those who know me well. My hunch is that I will receive some criticism for referencing my husband as much as I do in this book – a book about my career with the Raiders. It won't bother me one little bit if I do.

THERE WAS AN INSTANCE IN which I was prepared to resign.

Al observed the way I interacted with animals over the course of many years. Very early in my career, as he drove into the parking lot of our facility, he saw me sitting on the pavement playing with a stray cat. Another time, he saw me doing the same thing in the walkway between our football and administration buildings. On each of those occasions, he muttered in a voice clearly intended to be heard something about hoping that didn't bring us bad luck, noting in each instance that the cat was black. But each time, he stopped to look at the cat.

Early in my career, I learned that he too had a soft spot for animals, as one night, while he was being driven home from an event, he called me from the car. As we were speaking, I heard a loud thump. "What was that?" Al called to the driver. "It was a possum, Mr. Davis," I heard the driver respond. "Let's go back," I heard Al beseech the driver several times. "Let's see if we can help it." Al wanted to help the opossum.

Al also knew that I was an avid equestrian, as on most Saturdays, I came to the office straight from the barn and I both looked and smelled as if that was the case. On one such Saturday, Al called me as he was headed in to the office and asked me to join him in a meeting. I responded that I had come straight from the barn and wasn't dressed appropriately for a meeting. "Aw fuck, I don't care about that," Al responded, "I don't think of you that way." What a tremendous message to a young woman and new employee: he didn't care how I looked (or smelled) and he didn't think of me "that way."

Al also knew of my passion for animal rescue and of my work with Tony La Russa and his Animal Rescue Foundation.

In 2009, Al called me to discuss Michael Vick, who had been cleared to play following his indictment for dogfighting. There had been suggestions in the media that the Raiders were a perfect and likely spot for him to resume his career.

I was surprised that Al called me to discuss this, and I was also very touched, as his call suggested to me that not only was he cognizant of my views, but that he cared enough to elicit my thoughts and consider this subject with me.

Al raised the topic in a very direct manner and asked me my thoughts.

I told Al that I had read the indictment and that although the public discourse on this topic referenced dogfighting, what Vick was alleged to have done (and ultimately admitted he did) was exceedingly more horrific than anything I ever could or would have imagined. I also told Al that although the public discourse on this topic included commentary that dogfighting was acceptable in certain parts of the country, what Vick did was far more heinous than dogfighting (as bad as that is) and could in no way be justified based on norms. What Vick did was unspeakably cruel. He pled guilty to killing dogs with his own hands by drowning dogs and by hanging dogs. I also told Al that the indictment stated that his group committed unthinkable atrocities, including electrocuting some dogs and slamming others into the ground until they died. "What kind of person can kill a dog with his own hands?" I asked Al. As I was talking, Al was pleading with me, "No more, baby, please, please, no more, stop." His emotion was raw and palpable. He indicated that this topic was now closed; Michael Vick would not be a Raider.

I never shared with Al that prior to that conversation I had decided that if we did sign Michael Vick, I would resign. In fact, I had drafted my resignation letter, explaining why I would not remain with the organization were we to sign someone who committed such unspeakably cruel atrocities. I believe in second chances. One of the things that initially attracted me to the Raiders as a fan was the organization's tradition of providing second (and third and fourth) chances to those others would not. But I also believe it's a privilege to work in the NFL and to be a Raider. I believed that being a Raider mattered. I did not think that Michael Vick should be a Raider and I decided that were he to become one, I would not be his teammate. What was and shall always be so special to me is that Al initiated this conversation, that he sought my input before making any decision, and that he too concluded that this man should not be a Raider.

I ALSO ONCE OFFERED TO fire myself.

I had screwed something up. I considered it a big screw-up. I misjudged the human dynamics of a business situation and my mistake cost the organization approximately one million dollars, an amount that I considered very significant.

No one could have been angrier with me than I was with myself. I have always beaten myself up over what I believe to be my mistakes or misjudgments and when I believe that I could have handled something better than I did. I beat myself up far more and for far longer than anyone else has ever beaten me up for such things. I am more critical of myself than others are of me. I was inconsolable.

So, I approached Al to let him know that I had screwed up and that my misjudgment was costly. I waited for a quiet moment in hopes that I would have his full attention and wouldn't be rushed, and I went into his office and stated that we needed to discuss something. He briefly looked up from what he was doing. I think he understood that I wanted to raise a topic of serious importance to me – but he continued what he was doing and started telling me his observations about that afternoon's practice.

Every time he paused, I tried to change the topic and tell him about my screw-up. Finally, unable to wait any longer, I blurted out that I had made an enormous mistake in judgment that would cost the organization about a million dollars, and that I certainly understood he might decide to fire me.

He said nothing and kept working and talking. He asked me a few questions about ticket sales for the upcoming game, where we were in terms of profit and loss, the weather forecast for game day, and a few other things.

I answered all of his questions, and then tried again to explain my mistake, and what I believed to be its magnitude.

Without looking up, he said, "I heard you," and he continued what he was doing.

That was it. That was how he made clear that he was done with the discussion and, at least for the moment, with me.

The next day, I raised the topic again, again expressly stating that I fully understood that he might wish to terminate me, and that I would understand. He said nothing.

Finally, a day or two later, I went in and again raised the topic – only this time, I told him that to make this easier for him, I would fire myself. He finally looked up and said, "No one's firing you...you fucked up...it happens...I know you won't make this mistake again."

I had started walking out, and heard Al say one last thing: "You'll fuck up even bigger things."

And he was giggling. Yes, he giggled.

I ALSO ONCE OFFERED TO walk away, to make things easier for Al.

I have always embraced the concept of teamwork. I have never worked as what some describe as a lone wolf. When problem solving, looking for new ideas, attempting to engender creative thoughts, thinking through and addressing challenges, I gathered together varying groups of employees from varying departments and enlisted their participation. To the great chagrin of those who believed that there should be a "pecking order," I mixed senior staff with junior staff, as I thought that so doing was healthy and productive.

Some employees expressed to me that they thought I was too collaborative. I don't believe that to be the case, but if and to the extent that it was, I believe it preferable to err on the side of being too collaborative rather than not collaborative enough. Business is, in my view, best conducted as if it is a team sport. My teammates made me better than I otherwise would have been. I hope I made my teammates better than they otherwise would have been too.

Some people have suggested to me that collaboration is a distinctly feminine approach to doing business – an approach embraced only by leaders who are women – and that men are more likely to work as lone wolves. I don't agree with that. I have worked with women who are collaborative and women who are not. I have worked with men who are collaborative and men who are not. I also don't care whether it is true or not. Whether being collaborative is a "female approach" or not it is the approach that I like.

One of my coworkers was the antithesis of collaborative; he worked as that proverbial lone wolf. He was also very strategic in his efforts to advance himself. There were times I wished that I were more adept at such strategizing but after a bit of thought, I realized a few things: (a) not only wasn't I adept at it, I sucked at it; and (b) that was absolutely fine with me because I needed to follow my favorite words of advice: to thine own self be true.

I also don't think that time spent strategizing for one's own benefit is fair to one's employer. This employee spent what I considered an incomprehensible amount of time on such things and he was masterful at it. Most often, his efforts were at my expense. I know this because league office employees, employees of other clubs, and people in the media told me this. Eventually, Al told me that he too knew this.

It was brought to my attention on a number of occasions that this employee was working to persuade Al that he must select one of us (to wit: him) to be, or at least to be perceived as, Al's top advisor. I didn't take this personally; my presence was precluding him from getting what he wanted. Some people I respect have told me that this individual was comfortable engaging in the behavior he did because of my gender. I don't know if that was the case, but even if it was, that wasn't what concerned me. What concerned me was the effect his behavior was having on the organization.

Finally, after hearing about this for the umpteenth time and thinking again about how deleterious to the organization it was, I decided that enough was enough and I called Al to address this in the only manner I know how: directly.

When I called him and asked if he had a moment to speak, I sensed that he was in the middle of something, as he responded as he often did in those instances, with a brisk "What's up, kid?"

I told him that I was aware that this other employee wanted Al to make a "him or me" choice and I said: "I'll make this easy for you," and went on to say that if he thought that this employee would continue his efforts to force a choice, that if he believed as I did that those efforts were harmful to the organization, and if it would make things easier for him and be better for the organization, I would step away.

I wrote down Al's response verbatim and I still have the piece of paper on which I did so. I will keep it forever. He said: "Next time you call, make sure it's about something intelligent." He hung up without saying another word.

16
HE WOULDN'T LET US LOSE

AL DIED ON OCTOBER 8, 2011.

The call telling me he was gone came at about 3:20 AM. I was not surprised, yet I felt a sense of shock. I understood that I had to push aside the deep, profound sadness that was washing over and through me and collect myself, as there was so much I had to do. I called several of the Raiders' other owners and coworkers with whom I worked the most closely, and I called Roger Goodell. I don't remember precisely what Roger said, but I do remember that he was tremendously kind and compassionate.

We had a lot to do. We needed flights for Al's wife and son from Houston to Oakland and then a flight back to Houston for his son. We needed to alert everyone who was part of our organization, people who were close to the Raiders and some of Al's closest friends. We also needed to craft an appropriate statement to the public. There was so much to do.

Six hours went by and I hadn't slowed. Then, suddenly, I stopped for a moment and I burst into tears. I sobbed so hard that I couldn't speak and was barely able to breathe. In fact, I am crying now as I write this.

My husband was nearby at the time and I choked out these words to him: "Who is going to call me in the middle of the night and motherfuck me now?"

That was the first thing that I was able to articulate once the reality that Al was gone had set in. Al would have loved that.

As exasperating and infuriating as Al's dead-of-night, motherfucking phone calls were, I knew they were special. I also knew that I would miss them for the rest of my life. Now, years after his death, I still miss them terribly.

Very late that night, I flew to Houston. Our game the next day was surreal. The Texans understood how difficult this moment was and they offered a private area in which to watch the game. I invited a handful of other Raiders employees to join me if they wished to do so and we watched together.

Across the league, every stadium had a pregame moment of silence in Al's honor.

Late in the game, with just 2:56 left, we were winning by a slim margin of 25–20. At that point, I wanted to be on the field to watch the end of the game on the sideline with our team. I had never done that before, but on this day that just felt right. I told my coworkers with whom I was watching that I was headed to the field and I asked them to join me if they wished to do so.

We got to the field just as the Texans started their final possession. I was standing between the end of our bench and the end zone. The Texans were moving the ball easily. They had reached our 39-yard line with just under one minute remaining. On third-and-23, Texans quarterback Matt Schaub completed a pass down to our 5-yard line and then spiked the ball with only seven seconds left in the game. On the next play, Schaub moved to his left looking to throw. It seemed like he had hours. It appeared to me that Schaub had room to run but choose not to and instead attempted a pass.

I saw him throw the ball. I saw a Texans receiver who appeared to be wide open in the back of the end zone. *We lost the game*, I thought. *We lost the game*. I actually doubled over, so excruciating was the thought of losing.

Because I couldn't see over the photographers who were kneeling on the sideline I didn't see our safety, Michael Huff, who was in front of that receiver, as he was blocked from my view. Then, suddenly, I saw all of our players rushing to the end zone, throwing themselves on what I believed to be the ground. Only it wasn't the ground, it was Michael with the ball in his arms. I realized then that we won the game and I started crying very hard, as I am now. For a very brief moment I thought about running into the end zone and throwing myself onto Michael too – but I didn't. I simply cried and walked with the coaches, players, and others off the field and up the tunnel toward the locker room.

I found myself walking with Willie Brown. We clung to one another and cried.

The entire team was emotional after the game. Players were crying and our coach, Hue Jackson, sank to his knees, put his face in his hands, and also wept.

A day or so after the game, we were back at our facility, and I was at a lunch table in our dining area with Huff, our other starting safety Tyvon Branch, and a few other players who were on the field for that play. One of them noted that we only had 10 men on the field. He was right. I had seen one of our linebackers mistakenly run off before the play.

I shared my observation that the quarterback could have run into the end zone and that I couldn't believe that he didn't. Tyvon told me that when he saw our linebacker run off the field, he decided that he would follow Schaub and that if Schaub was going to run, he was going to have to go through him.

We were finished eating but before leaving the table, I told the players we didn't have 10 men on the field; we had 11. A few corrected me. One player started to explain which linebacker mistakenly went off the field right before the snap. I shook my head no, and again said that we had 11 men on the field. Michael and Tyvon understood what I meant.

"No, she's right, we had 11," one of them said.

There is no way Al would let us lose that game.

SOURCES

Publications

Keynes, John Maynard. *The General Theory of Employment, Interest and Money*. (Palgrave Macmillan, 1935).

Websites

WSJ.com
SI.com